THE
HOLLYWOOD
COMMANDMENTS

THE
HOLLYWOOD
COMMANDMENTS

A SPIRITUAL GUIDE TO SECULAR SUCCESS

DeVON
FRANKLIN

WITH TIM VANDEHEY

HarperOne
An Imprint of HarperCollinsPublishers

FIRST EDITION

Designed by Yvonne Chan

Library of Congress Cataloging-in-Publication Data
Names: Franklin, DeVon, author.
Title: The Hollywood commandments : a spiritual guide to secular success / DeVon Franklin.
Description: FIRST EDITION. | San Francisco : HarperOne, 2017.
Identifiers: LCCN 2017022888 | ISBN 9780062684257 (hardcover) | ISBN 9780062803245 (B&N signed edition) | ISBN 9780062695024 (audio)
Subjects: LCSH: Success—Religious aspects—Christianity.
Classification: LCC BV4598.3 .F728 2017 | DDC 248.4—dc23
LC record available at https://lccn.loc.gov/2017022888

17 18 19 20 21   LSC   10 9 8 7 6 5 4 3 2 1

This book is dedicated to everyone who wants to be free.
Free to be who God created you to be and
do everything you were created to do.
To those who want to go further than you ever thought possible
in achieving your God-ordained destiny.
To those who are tired of living beneath your potential and
crave the success you know is within your grasp.
To those who want peace in the depths of your spirit . . .
this book is for you.

CONTENTS

WHAT THE CHURCH DOESN'T TEACH YOU ABOUT SUCCESS

I was basking in the afterglow of one the biggest successes of my career when God spoke to me and told me it was time to "get out of the boat." It was the spring of 2014, and the movie *Heaven Is for Real,* starring Greg Kinnear, had just shocked Hollywood by making almost $30 million in its first five days. I was senior vice president of production for Columbia Pictures, a division of Sony Pictures Entertainment, where I had been an executive for nearly ten years, and I staked my career on my belief that *Heaven Is for Real* would be a box office hit.

I came to Hollywood because I wanted to be a producer and make entertainment filled with faith and hope—entertainment that could inspire the world like *Heaven Is for Real*. I wanted to do that by running my own production company. I never had the desire to work long-term as a studio executive, and in that moment, I realized that God had been using my time as an executive to prepare me to run my own company one day. Apparently, that day had come sooner than I thought! As I felt that nudge in my spirit to "get out of the boat," I knew what it meant: *I had to quit my job.*

In the book of Matthew in the New Testament, there's a famous story that has always inspired me. It's the story of Peter getting out of the boat to walk on water to Jesus. Jesus had sent his disciples out on a boat to sail the Sea of Galilee after they had finished ministering and while he went up to the mountaintop to pray. When he finished praying, it was the middle of the night, and he walked on water toward the disciples' boat. When they saw Jesus walking on water, it scared them so much they thought he was a ghost. Jesus said (Matthew 14:27–29, NLT), "Don't be afraid . . . take courage. I am here." But Peter was the only discile to speak up and challenge this claim, saying, "Lord, if it's really you, tell me to come to you, walking on water." Jesus said, "Yes, come." In that moment, Peter got out of the boat and did the impossible: he stepped onto the water and walked toward Jesus.

This story was the perfect metaphor for what I was feeling because I was constantly praying, "Lord, do you have more for me? Is the dream you gave me ever going to happen?" In this moment, it was as if Jesus was saying, "Come." But it also stopped me in my tracks. I realized that my studio executive job was the boat, and Jesus was my dream. In order for me to reach my dream, I was going to have to step completely out of my job. I was going to have to risk everything.

That's the scariest thing about the story of Peter walking on water: he had no guarantee that the water would hold him. He risked drowning. He had to have faith that if Jesus was calling him to do this, somehow the water would transform underneath his feet into a firm surface he could walk on and not drown. But he wouldn't know until he stepped out of the boat onto it. Peter had to make a leap of faith. In the same way, I wouldn't know if I would fail or succeed until I had the faith to step out of my own boat and quit.

CALLED TO DO MORE

Have you been there? Felt like God was calling you to something more, something maybe a little scary and unfamiliar but that would take you a step further into your purpose, your destiny? We all have at one time or another. It's always unexpected, and it can be confusing. There's no manual or set of rules that tells you what to do when God taps you on the shoulder and whispers, "It's time to make a move." You might feel fear, exhilaration, or both at the same time. I know, because that's how I felt. So, believe me, I get it.

On Easter Sunday, I got an email from the chairman of Sony Pictures, Amy Pascal, that read, "I hope you're feeling great!" I was. It was the second email she sent me over the weekend congratulating me on the success of *Heaven Is for Real*. I felt something stir in my spirit when I got this email, and that's when I heard God say, loudly and clearly, "It's time to go, you've got to get out of the boat."

So instead of just replying back to Amy's email by saying, "Yes, I'm feeling great," I took this opportunity to seize the moment. I asked her if we could have a meeting. She replied, "Yes, definitely."

On the day of the meeting, I nervously walked down to Amy's office and waited for her to finish a call. Then her assistant said, "Amy is ready to see you," and my heart was beating out of my chest. Amy is a force of nature, one of the most successful people in the history of Hollywood. She greeted me warmly and congratulated me again on the success of the movie. I sat down on the couch, mustered as much courage as I could, and said, "I love you and love Sony, but it's time for me to go."

Surprised, she said, "What do you mean?"

"It's been a blessing to be here and help create value for the company for almost ten years," I said. "However, I can't keep creating value that I'm unable to participate in. I came to Hollywood to start my own production company, and I know now is the time to do it."

There was a beat of silence, and I knew it was my chance to add the kicker:

"And I want Sony to fund it. I want you to give me a first-look deal so I can start my own company."

Whew! Scripture says, "So let us come boldly to the throne of our gracious God" (Hebrews 4:16, NLT). God gives us the authority to come before Him boldly to ask for what we need, so why be afraid to go boldly before a man or woman to ask for what we need? In other words, step up and ask! So, I did.

Amy looked at me for a long moment, and finally she said, "Well, okay. Yes, I'll do it! We value the contributions you've made to this company, and we don't want you leaving this studio. So, we'll give you a deal under one condition: you can't negotiate with anybody else."

I quickly replied, "Okay, as long as the deal is good." She laughed, we hugged, and I walked out of her office practically walking on water myself.

DESTINATION: DESTINY

Talk about stepping out on faith! I had no idea whether it was going to work or whether Amy would say yes. But I wasn't concerned. It was time. Too often we ignore the alarm that goes off in our spirit when it's time to make a career or life move; instead, we keep hitting the snooze button. How many people have snoozed away their destiny? I refuse to be less than I was created to be, and I endeavor every day to discover who I really am and to achieve the destiny God has promised me. I also felt the way everyone feels—the way *you* feel—when you're stuck in a job that doesn't fulfill you. You know you can be more and do more, but you're afraid. There's the mortgage and the car and the kids and the uncertainty . . . and before long, practicality suffocates your purpose.

When those choices confront us, we have to ask ourselves a question. Do we want our gravestone to read, "Lived a properly practical life," or "Lived a life of passionate purpose"? I know what I want carved on mine. When you decide that following your purpose passionately is the most important thing, you break out every skill, every bit of wisdom, and every character strength at your disposal, and you *go for it.*

During this time, I realized something revelatory. The skill set, knowledge, and wisdom that I was relying on to enable my transformation into a film and TV producer—industry understanding, creative competency, marketing and publicity knowledge, political maneuvering, contract negotiation—were *not* qualities that I had developed in church! Even though I've been a Christian all my life and grown up in the church, a place that shaped my character, my worldview, and my faith, I didn't learn those lessons there. I learned them in Hollywood, in what some people would call "the belly of the beast." Yet those Hollywood-honed skills were what would help me achieve my destiny and live according to God's will.

GOD'S POWER DOESN'T STOP AT THE GATES OF HOLLYWOOD

Does having faith make you less successful? Do Biblical principles work against secular success? Does God care if you are a spiritual success but a secular failure? Is it possible for spiritual teachings and secular strategies to work in concert not only to help you achieve the success you've been yearning for but also to help you become who you are destined to be?

As I said, I was raised in the church, but we never addressed those kinds of questions. Almost every single weekend of my upbringing was spent on a pew singing worship songs and listening to the pastor preach. As a young teen, I was deeply moved and convicted to accept Christ as my personal savior. As I came into adolescence, I believed what I was taught: I can do all things through Christ Jesus who strengthens me, and all things are possible to those who believe.

Then something interesting happened. As I began to express my belief that God wanted me to live out my calling by working in Hollywood and the entertainment business, I was met not only with blank stares but with admonitions:

"Hollywood is the Devil's playground!"

"Hollywood is Sodom and Gomorrah!"

"It's not a place for Christians."

"You will lose your faith."

I was perplexed. How could God's power stop at the gates of Hollywood? Was it possible that there is actually a limit to what our faith in Him can do? If we commit our lives to Him, does that limit how far our God-given ambitions can take us?

There was also an undercurrent of fear running through those warnings. It's part of a culture of fear—a *beware* mentality—that is taught and widely reinforced within the community of believers. Generations of well-meaning Christians who felt alarm bells going off in their spirits urging them to live out their calling in the secular world—to *glorify* God by achieving worldly success—chose not to pursue their destiny because the church convinced them they would *go too far* or *lose their faith*. Because of this, many never experienced the fullness of their lives—and in turn, missed out on the fullness of God.

It's common to characterize the entertainment industry this way, but many industries are subject to similar thinking, including the high-tech world, professional sports, and politics. Maybe you've been told something similar about a career path or lifestyle you're pursuing. This fear of being *outside God's grace* has been used too often to control and curtail bold, radical faith—faith that was *designed* to thrive in the secular world and to transform that world, and us in the process! I believe that is why so many people are secretly unfulfilled—especially people of faith.

As I began looking for answers to these problems, I again went to the scriptures. One of the most compelling stories I found, one that I felt might hold the secret answers to this dilemma, was the story of Daniel, Shadrach, Meshach, and Abednego in Babylon.

THE LESSONS OF BABYLON

In the Bible, Daniel 1 tells the story of the Israelites: Daniel, Shadrach, Meshach, and Abednego (popularly known as the Hebrew Boys). Given internships in the kingdom of Babylon, these young men were fit, healthy, handsome, and quick studies. They were the best of what Israel had to offer. But as they began to serve in Babylon, they were met with a serious conflict: the king had assigned them a diet that did not align with their Hebrew beliefs.

As foreigners, they felt confident they could do the job at hand, yet they had no idea if Babylon's rules could be adapted to fit their faith. Should they compromise what they believed in to fit into their new careers or stand firm on their convictions and risk not only conflict but potential death?

They decided to make a very savvy move. Rather than recuse themselves from doing the job, they asked if they could do it differently. Daniel and the Hebrew Boys asked their supervisor if they could eat their own diet (consisting of vegetables and water). However, the supervisor worried that if he granted their request he would lose his job and refused. Undeterred, they then asked the guard who managed them daily. They said, "If you give us a chance to eat differently for ten days, we will prove that we can fulfill the requirements of our job. If we can't, we will suffer the consequences." The guard agreed.

Ten days later, the Hebrew Boys were better nourished and healthier than any of the other interns, so the guard allowed them to continue on with their diet. Ultimately, when it was time for them to be brought before the king, they were found to be ten times healthier and better at their jobs than all their peers.

The takeaway is simple yet profound:

> **They learned in Babylon how to be successful in a secular environment by applying their spirituality in a way that enhanced their success.**

The Hebrew Boys learned how to succeed while at work in Babylon, *not in the synagogue*. Some of the lessons they learned:

- Don't be afraid of "No." "No" sets you up for the right "Yes."

- Passion persuades.

- Being different is a divine asset.

- Risk-averse is success-averse.

- People will either view you as a threat or asset to their job security.

- Results matter. The bottom line counts.

- Persistence is essential.

- Sacrifice is your salvation.

- God will show up on the job He's placed you in but only if you put Him to the test.

- Adhering to your spiritual beliefs powers your secular ascent.

The story of the Hebrew Boys as told throughout the book of Daniel inspired me. It helped me find the courage to pursue a career in Hollywood while adhering to my Christian beliefs. And just like the Hebrew Boys, I've learned more about success in the secular world of Hollywood than I ever did in the church.

Hollywood has revealed a more dynamic picture of God than I ever saw within the confines of the church walls. In twenty years in the entertainment business, I've learned some of the most surprising and important lessons about God's intention for our success. Those lessons have enabled me to build an amazing life and thriving career that glorifies God, whether I'm working on a movie set, meeting with celebrities, collaborating with directors, or negotiating with agents.

In fact, I'll go so far as to say something that might get me kicked out of a few churches:

The church didn't teach me how to be successful. Hollywood did.

In the church, we learn vital spiritual knowledge that shapes our values and morals, determines how we see the world, reveals who we are in relation to God, and shows us His plan for our salvation. Yet when it comes time to apply that spiritual knowledge to meet practical demands, there's a huge question left unanswered: "How do I apply what I believe to what I do professionally?"

Like the Hebrew Boys, I've learned the secrets to success in Babylon, incredibly valuable lessons about how each of us can succeed in life while enjoying the success God intends for us to have. It doesn't matter if you're in Hollywood or a completely different profession—these principles will transform your life by empowering you with truth, clarity, and strategy you can use to leap forward into the fullness of your calling.

THE HOLLYWOOD COMMANDMENTS

This isn't a book about Hollywood elites by a Hollywood elite. No, this book is about *your* success! Too often, we salivate over the lives of celebrities and voyeuristically covet their lives at the expense of our own. Your life can shine brighter than any star in Hollywood but only if you let it! No matter if you are a dentist, an accountant, a teacher, a small business owner, a lawyer, a firefighter, or a stay-at-home parent, my hope is that these principles, these Commandments, will guide you to the thriving life that God has uniquely set in front of *you*.

For more than one hundred years, Hollywood has endured as one of the most influential industries in the world, influencing every aspect of global culture. No matter the economic conditions, the political forces, or cultural shifts—the entertainment industry has endured. Why is this relevant to you? Because I've identified universal tips, tools, and strategies from my time in Hollywood that can help you become a long-lasting success, no matter what walk of life you're in. If there are challenges and doubts that keep you up late at night, how do you resolve them? If there are politics and rivalries that are impeding your progress, how do you navigate them? If there are rules and bureaucracies limiting your ascension, how do you understand what they are and how they work so you can become more effective? I will share the answers to these questions based on what I've learned in Hollywood.

One common misunderstanding is that the majority of people in the entertainment industry are rich, famous stars. Not true. The vast majority of entertainment professionals are hardworking people who perform very specific jobs behind the scenes. They're on-set electricians and location scouts. They're makeup artists and production company accountants. They're studio musicians and drivers. Their work isn't glamorous, and they don't walk red carpets, but they make the entertainment business go. These Commandments are geared to make your life, career, and success go, too, no matter what you do to earn your daily bread!

Let's be clear about one thing. If your goal is to get the house of a lifetime, the car of your dreams, or more money than you know how to handle, *this book is not for you*! I don't care if you ever drive a Bentley, own a private jet, carry a Birkin bag, or buy a mansion in the hills. What I care about is seeing you live out your God-given purpose in this life, walk in your calling, and unleash the full power of your gifts. If you feel stuck in your career, feel a deep sense that there's more to life than the life you're living, or if you are just looking for information about how to get to the next level of your calling, then *this book is for you.*

I define success as a deep sense of peace, and we find the most peace when we live out our true calling and fulfill the purpose we were created for. History is filled with examples of people who had an abundance of material possessions but no peace because no matter how much stuff you have, there's not enough money in the world to fill the hole in your soul. That's not the fate I want for you. I want to help you become the person you're destined to be.

The key lesson: you can be wildly successful in a secular world without losing your faith. A secular world is one that is not overtly religious, and whether we like it or not, this is the world most of us live in most of the time. But if you make the right choices, your success in the secular world can actually *strengthen* your faith. I'm proof of that. Too many people believe that "worldly" success contradicts the principles of faith, but the opposite is true. Faith will not hold you back from success; it will *empower* it. The truth is, you may never fully experience God unless you fully pursue the secular ambitions He placed deep in your spirit. After all, He put them there for a reason!

In Daniel, God never condemns the fact that his people are working in Babylon. He uses Babylon as a tool to demonstrate how great He is—how universal and effective the ideas that come from His teachings are. When you live by your spiritual principles and enjoy secular success, you're actually doing a service to the God you claim to worship.

God never meant for His people to hermetically seal themselves within the church. The principles the Hebrew Boys applied to their success came out of their desire to be successful spiritually. If they had stuck to what they had learned in the synagogue, they would never have achieved true success.

God wants us to ground ourselves in profound spirituality and faith and then venture boldly into our careers. Think of it as a spiritual version of the *Star Trek* motto: "To boldly go where no believer has gone before!" Life is a beautiful adventure, and you can't be afraid to explore! It's time to live your freest and truest possible life!

A USER'S MANUAL

The Hollywood Commandments is the user's manual to doing exactly that. It's based on the most important lessons I've picked up during my career in Hollywood as a successful producer and believing Christian. These lessons—a.k.a. "Commandments"—are the heart of the book and are relevant to any industry, from academics to tech to business to entrepreneurship:

1. Your Prayers Alone Aren't Enough

2. You Are the Talent

3. You Have to Carry a Crown Before You Can Wear One

4. You Have to Know the Rules to Play the Game

5. Your Gut Is Hiding God

6. You Get What You Negotiate (Not What You're Worth)

7. You Must Master the Walk of Fame

8. Your Difference Is Your Destiny

9. Your Amnesia Is an Asset

10. Your World Is Smaller Than You Think

What I have found is that, contrary to what people of faith often believe, as you invest more of yourself in your career, spiritual wisdom becomes *more* relevant, not less. Character, wisdom, values, sense of purpose—the more you hope to achieve, the more they are the bedrock of what you *can* achieve. But by themselves, they are not enough. My time in Hollywood has shown me that, while God might reveal to you your passionate purpose, it's still up to you to go after it. That means you have to do a lot more than heed God's call, show up on the job, and say, "Here I am!"

In his critically acclaimed book *The Tipping Point*, *New York Times* bestselling author and thought leader Malcolm Gladwell says we have to put in ten thousand hours to master anything. To me, that's code for *you have to be obsessed with what you do*. Learn the skills, test your talents, and practice your purpose continuously. Being who God is calling you to be will take everything you've got: your spirit, physicality, emotion, everything. You have to push, and you have to push, and then you have to push some more. Reaching your dream is always harder than you think it's going to be. The world does not give up what you want easily. It gives it up grudgingly. God will inspire, guide, teach, and reveal. But He won't do the work for you.

This book is a user's manual for balancing the secular and the spiritual and for understanding how each fits into the other. The balance is that place where ambition meets accountability and what you want for your life meets what God wants for you. We'll learn about understanding the rules behind that balance—the Commandments—and putting them to work in your life.

Why life? Because life should be about more than how to earn a living. It should be about how to achieve the fullest expression of who we really are. Achieving that is one of the greatest ways to honor God. Does that mean you have to leave your job, start a business, or go for the promotion? Yes, it might! Does it mean you have to compromise in your faith? Definitely not. The Bible famously says that faith without works is dead, and that means that faith with works is *life*. True success means learning how faith and work fit together.

1

YOUR PRAYERS ALONE AREN'T ENOUGH

Prayer does not change God, but it changes him who prays.
—Soren Kierkegaard

My wife, Meagan Good, is an actress who has enjoyed a tremendous and fulfilling career in entertainment. Last year she felt compelled to embark upon a new goal: become an action star. However, Meagan is very petite. And while she's been a leading lady most of her career, she hasn't done many action roles. Most people in Hollywood didn't see her as the action-movie type, which created a dilemma. She needed to change how directors, producers, and casting directors saw her, and that meant one thing: changing herself physically.

To be clear, nothing was or is wrong with Meagan's body. Action stars simply require a certain level of physicality and fitness to be successful and credible. While all action stars have stunt doubles, they still do a good portion of their stunts, which mandates they be in peak physical condition. Meagan hadn't ever trained for that level of physicality or fitness before.

She prayed about her goal and asked God for confirmation. She believed God had spoken in her spirit and told her that action films were the next stage in her career. However, I would come home from work and see her on the couch eating junk food. When I asked her if she had gone to the gym, she would have an excuse for why she hadn't gone on that particular day. This pattern repeated itself often. Then one day she was expressing her frustration that, while she had been praying consistently, she wasn't receiving opportunities to go out for action parts. I was a little nervous to tell her what I was thinking, but I hoped she would receive it in the love with which I intended it. I turned to her and gently said, "You have to prepare for what you are praying for. You can't expect God's promises to manifest in your life if you aren't getting ready for them." It took her a minute to respond, but once it sunk in, she agreed.

Since we've been together, Meagan has never liked the gym. But in order to prepare for what she was praying for, she had to do something she didn't want to do: work out regularly. She had no gym membership, gym clothes, or workout program, so she got them. She started to go to the gym, take Tae Kwon Do classes, and get up early every morning to exercise. After a while, she started saying things like, "I love working out," and, "I don't feel right if a day passes and I haven't worked out." When I heard that I'd think, "Who is this new woman in my wife's body?" I couldn't imagine that a person who hated working out so much had become so obsessed with it.

Before long, the work started to pay off. Meagan started to transform physically, and she began to look like the action star she wanted to be. She became lean and muscular and learned to throw a spinning back kick that could knock a grown man back five feet. People began to ask her if she was preparing for a role, and she would reply, "Yes, I already have it; it just hasn't manifested yet." Finally, after months of preparing and working, Meagan got the opportunity to be the new Foxy Brown, an iconic female action character dedicated to protecting those who can't protect themselves. It's being developed as a TV series for Hulu.

AN IDEA THAT MIGHT GET ME KICKED OUT OF CHURCH

Prayer is important. It's the cornerstone of our relationship with God, our private time with the Creator. Now, let's look at why preparing and taking action is as important as praying. To some people raised in the church, this idea is straight-up blasphemy, which is why I said that it might get me booted out of—or at least, politely disinvited to speak at—a few churches. I was raised in the faith, and we're taught that the Lord is all-powerful and can achieve anything for those who have faith in Him. And that's all true. But just because God can do anything doesn't mean that he *should* . . . or that he *will*.

This builds on an idea I discussed in my first book, *Produced by Faith*. Think about the relationship between parents and children. If you're a parent, it's your job to love your kids, protect them, be an example of discipline, compassion, and wisdom, help them develop intellectually and spiritually, and put them in situations where they can learn strength, self-esteem, and faith. It's *not* your job to do everything for them or give them everything they want. Sure, you could buy them a fancy car when they turn sixteen, and you could do all their homework for them so they never get a grade below an A. But what happens to kids who never learn the value of doing things for themselves? *Exactly.* They grow up spoiled, entitled, and helpless.

Well, we're all God's children, and because He is a great parent, He doesn't do everything for us. Preparation is for our benefit and edification. Preparation is also bold faith in action. You pray because you believe God is going to do what you've prayed for. If God had sent Meagan a fantastic part in an action movie before she was prepared for it, she probably wouldn't have valued it when it arrived, and she would have been unprepared to take it on because she lacked the physicality she needed to be successful. God brings us insight, inspiration, strength, and relationships with people who can help us. But we have to put in the work and prepare so that when the harvest comes, we're ready.

In other words:

Your Prayers Alone Aren't Enough

Prayer is the way we communicate with God and learn what path he wants us to take. However, what I learned from Meagan's experience is that while getting what you want should always *begin* with prayer, if you actually want to see results you can't stop at prayer. Anything you are praying for you must also *prepare* for.

We all want the harvest because harvest time is sweet! We want our season of reaping and enjoying the fruits of our labor, yet we spend too much time either complaining about why it hasn't come yet or getting frustrated with the amount of work required to produce it. In the end, one of two things happens: we don't get the harvest at all, or when harvest time comes we are incapable of maximizing it because we didn't prepare for it in advance.

We're all anticipating something good coming to us in our careers—advancement, a big opportunity, or even a new career path. But while you're waiting for this thing to come to pass, please prepare. Pray that God will lead you to your destiny. Pray for opportunities that align with your true self. Absolutely, pray and seek His will in everything. Yet when prayer is done, get up and put in the work. Every day I pray then I go to work! I work on becoming a better speaker, a better author, a better producer, a better businessman, a better husband, a better friend, and so on.

False Idols

When does furious intensity to succeed become something to criticize instead of admire? When it compels you to compromise what is right. Doing something illegal or immoral for the sake of advancement can derail God's purpose for you because doing it turns you into someone else—someone different from the person you were created to be. So, a short-term compromise for the sake of the high-speed rush to get results can lead you down the slippery slope. At the bottom, you won't find success but shame and loss.

PRAY AND PREPARE

Make "Pray and Prepare" your personal motto. Prayer is only the beginning of the process. God told me I was going to be a producer when I was a child, but that purpose took years to manifest, and it didn't manifest just because I prayed. I had to move from Northern California to Los Angeles. I not only attended college at the University of Southern California but also maintained an internship and sometimes held down two jobs while being a full-time student. I had to get up every day and put in work on my skills, grow my understanding of the industry, and build relationships.

It took eighteen years from the time I set foot in Los Angeles to the day I closed my first producing deal! That's 6,570 days, 157,680 hours of preparation. Each day I would pray to God for it to happen, and then I'd prepare myself for when it did happen by pushing myself to learn everything there was to learn about what He was calling me to do. By the time my harvest came, I was ready for it. Everything I went through up to that point was necessary to prepare my heart, my integrity, and my ability to manage the harvest when it was time.

Why do so many people think that prayer is enough to achieve their highest purpose? I think there are three main reasons:

1. **Fatalism.** Among some of the faithful, you can find a dangerous kind of fatalism—a belief that we don't have the power to change things in our life, so all we have to do is just ask God for something and then sit back and wait for Him to bring it to us. That's treating God like He's a genie, and we've rubbed a magic lamp, or like prayers are spiritual quarters for God's vending machine. But God doesn't work that way. If you pray to Him for something that's beyond your power to produce—healing for a loved one who's gravely ill, for instance—He can and often does deliver miracles. But when something is very much within your power to manifest, like researching the industry you desire to work in or putting in a resume with a company you admire, God's more likely to say, "What are you asking Me for? Go and get it done!"

2. **The "in this world but not of this world" doctrine.** As Christians, we are sometimes warned that we should live separate from the secular world. The reason is that the world outside the church walls is evil and could aggressively turn us against God—so much so that we should fear going "too deep" into the world. Based on this line of thinking, is it okay to be ambitious about a career outside the confines of what the church deems accept-

able? No, sir! We were taught that was something that would tempt us and draw us further away from God.

I believe we're commissioned by God to be the instruments of His Word in the world, and what better way to do that than by living according to the values of our faith in our careers and lives, where we can have the greatest effect on other people through our words and actions? Even Jesus says, "I'm not asking you to take them out of the world, but to keep them safe from the evil one" (John 17:15, NLT). I developed the ambition to go into entertainment specifically because I felt that God's purpose for me was to help bring change to the world through film and television—the most powerful communications media on earth.

There is nothing ungodly about focusing on your career or having strong career ambitions, as long as those ambitions don't distance you from the values of your faith. Don't be afraid to go after every good thing God has put in your heart to pursue, even if it doesn't line up with other people's vision for you.

3. **We obsess over the end result and forget to value the process.** For me, the process looks like this. My day of rest is the Sabbath, so from Friday night sundown to Saturday night sundown I go to church and recover from the stresses of a tough week. When Sunday comes around, it's time for me to get ready for the week ahead. On a typical Sunday, my first workout might be at eight in the morning. Then I'll usually check out a sermon online. I might have a call with a screenwriter to give them notes on a project or have a script I need to read. I'll get my wife's car and my car washed, go to the grocery store, sometimes get in a second workout in the afternoon, then carve out time to spend with Meagan if she's not working.

None of those activities helps me to magically arrive at the fulfillment of my goals. But that's not why I do all that stuff. To go back to the harvest metaphor, it's easy to focus all your attention on the vegetables you're going to reap in the autumn. But if you do that, then you'll neglect the planting, watering, fertilizing, and weeding—the maintenance—that makes the harvest possible. We love results, but we hate waiting for them. When you set about transforming your body in the gym, and you work out for a month, you're not going to see results. If you work out for six months, you'll see some results, but you won't see the fullness of those results. It might take a year or more to manifest the results you have in your mind today. In life, we often quit too early. We put in minimum effort and expect maximum return. Receiving the best life and career don't work like that.

If you don't learn to fully commit to the process required for success, you will never achieve all the results the process can yield. If you just pray and do half the work, you're never going to achieve the fullness of your purpose.

To be who you're called to be and do what you're called to do will take everything within you: your energy, your spirit, your body, your mind, and your emotion.

Remember what I said: you have to push, and push, and push, and push some more. Pushing strengthens you and unlocks the power within you—and let's face it, you need that power because the world is tough and it *pushes back*.

The world does not give up what we want easily. This journey to fulfillment is not for the faint of heart. There will be roadblocks in your way, and when you clear one, there will be another, and another. You have to be *relentless* and keep doing the right things day after day without worrying too much about the reward. Put in the time, commit 100 percent to the process, and the rewards will come. Because the stronger, more determined, more focused, smarter person you're becoming? *That's* a reward in and of itself.

SETBACKS ARE SETUPS

All careers, without exception, are exercises in enduring phases of learning and acclimation. Michael Jordan didn't start out as the greatest player in NBA history (sorry Curry, Kobe, and LeBron fans, I still believe Jordan is the greatest); he became that person through years of work and overcoming what seemed like setbacks, including being cut from his high school varsity team as a sophomore because he was only five feet ten. It's true. In fact, when Michael was inducted into the Naismith Memorial Basketball Hall of Fame, he not only credited that particular setback for determining his lifelong work ethic, he even invited Leroy Smith, the six-foot-seven player who took his spot on the varsity squad, to attend the ceremony.

Michael celebrated the setback because he knew it was really a setup that helped lay the foundation for his eventual success. That early disappointment taught him as a young man that if he wanted to be ready to achieve his full purpose, he would have to push through adversity and keep believing in who he knew he could be even in the face of circumstances trying to tell him otherwise.

The big problem with setbacks is that we often look at them without a spiritual perspective. When we do that, we only see failures or disappointments as setbacks that take us further away from our goals. Discouragement makes us doubt God and ourselves. We ask, "If God loves me so much, why would He allow me to fail? Why was I stupid enough to believe I could have what I want?" When we can't reconcile the God we believe in with the life we believe we are destined to live, disappointment can take up permanent residence in our lives, detouring us indefinitely and leading to years of bitter unhappiness.

Now, try an experiment. Look at everything in the last year of your life that you've labeled as a setback and relabel it as a "setup" divinely designed to help you achieve your purpose. What do I mean? Think of Joseph in the Bible. He dreamt of one day being a ruler, but every step toward that dream seemed to become a setback that took him further away from its realization. He was sold into slavery by his brothers, falsely accused and thrown in jail, and forgotten in jail by the person he helped. However, once the dream was fulfilled, and Joseph became a ruler in Egypt, it became clear that the struggles and setbacks he faced along the way were in fact setups designed specifically to help him achieve his dream.

Setups prepare us to serve God's full purpose in our careers. If God had made me a producer when I was right out of college, I wouldn't have known what to do. I had no knowledge. I had no experience. Excelling in anything requires time to learn and to apprentice, and that's especially true in entertainment, which is an apprenticeship business. You learn by doing under the watchful eye of those who have more experience than you do. It was that way before I got to Hollywood, and it's still that way today.

God places setups in your path so that by the time you make it through them, you've become someone who can do the job in any capacity—who can lead and excel. By the time you pass the bar, get your teaching certificate, or reach the corner office, you're ready, and you know what to do with the opportunity. You know how to maximize your potential, manage your time, and build alliances. It shocks me to this day how prepared I am to run my production company, Franklin Entertainment. Every day, it requires a piece of wisdom that I didn't even realize that I was going to need, but I have it because I went through the process of setups at every stage of my career—intern, assistant, junior executive, senior executive, and producer—to acquire it.

My former colleague Pete Nowalk is a great example of this. When I was an executive at Sony Pictures, Pete was the assistant to the president of production, Matt Tolmach. Pete was always excellent at his job and incredibly accommodating with the needs various executives would have. Even though Pete was an assistant, he had dreams of one day becoming a writer. One of the benefits of working for the president of production is that all the scripts the studio is making come across your desk. Pete would read as many scripts as he could get his hands on, and then he started writing his own scripts on the side. One of those scripts eventually caught the attention of Shonda Rhimes, one of the most successful showrunners in television, and her ShondaLand production company. Pete left his job as an assistant and worked under Shonda for six years—first, as a writer on *Private Practice*, then *Grey's Anatomy*, and ultimately, as a co–executive producer and writer on *Scandal*.

One day Pete came up with his own idea for a show about a group of ambitious law students and their genius criminal defense professor who become involved in a twisted murder plot that changes their lives forever. This idea became the hit ABC TV show called *How to Get Away with Murder,* one of the highest-rated and most talked about shows on television. Pete is the showrunner, and not only does he oversee the creative content of the show, he's also responsible for overseeing all the writers on the show, working with the actors, and deciding on directors, interacting with the ABC network executives.

It's a full-time job that requires every aspect of his skills. All his years as an assistant prepared him by helping him develop the leadership and creative skills he now uses every day.

Everything you're going through in your life right now is preparing you to do what you've dreamed about. Prayer helps us know that we're on the right path and inspires us to keep going. When we don't look past the setups and the process but learn to cherish them, God gives us the means to achieve excellence in whatever field we choose.

Exodus

There are many well-meaning people who will insist that in order to get what you want, all you need to do is just work and prayer has no impact. Your prayers as an extension of your faith combined with your work are what produces the results. The path to success is as much spiritual as it is practical, and if you're listening to someone who keeps trying to persuade you to drop the spiritual side of your success pursuit, then you might be better served by reducing that person's influence on your life. It's tempting to think that "we can do it all by our strength," but true success is a combination of divine guidance and purpose and old-fashioned effort and persistence.

DO YOUR PART

How do I know this? After *The Pursuit of Happyness,* and before *The Karate Kid,* I was at a low at Sony. I thought I was trying to live according to what God wanted me to do, but it felt like there was something missing. While my career was good, I didn't feel like I was being who

I was supposed to be. I didn't feel valued. I didn't feel like I mattered at all. I felt replaceable. I felt lost.

At that time, I was praying, showing up at work, and saying, "Okay, God, I trust you're going to work it out, but when is it going to happen?" Nothing changed, and I began to realize that maybe things were the way they were not because God wasn't answering or wasn't concerned but because *I wasn't doing my part*. What was my excuse? I had the education. I had the relationships. I had the job. What was stopping me from going after the things God had promised me? I had been assuming God was just going to manifest new stages in my career. But remember what I wrote earlier:

**God doesn't give us what we have the
power to get for ourselves.**

That's a big, uncomfortable idea. God wants us to grow and become our best selves, and sometimes that only happens when we face adversity. I started to realize that maybe I had to go beyond prayer, beyond just waiting for God, and act. Now, I believe that there are times that you have to wait for God, but there are also certain times where you have to be active. You wait on God when you need insight, when you need to know His purpose for you, and what He wants of you. I already knew that; God had told me. But there I was, still waiting. However, the waiting season was over, and when I figured that out and started taking decisive action, things started to change.

There's one more reason not to rely solely on prayer: you run the risk of weakening your faith. Now, I know you're saying, "DeVon, how in the world can prayer weaken my faith?" If we don't think it's going to take everything we have, combined with prayer, to be successful, we can wind up putting too much on God. When we outsource our responsibility for our own lives and put everything on God, we create an expectation that can result in devastation. Because while God will do His work, He's not going to do the work we're supposed to do for ourselves! If our prayer life creates an unwarranted expectation that God will do it all, and then He doesn't, that disappointment can prove devastating for our faith. We need a strong prayer life to gain God's insight and motivation, but we also need a strong work ethic to make God's purpose for our lives a reality.

One of my greatest inspirations is Dwayne "The Rock" Johnson. His story and lifestyle are a source of pure motivation. Johnson is arguably the biggest movie star in the world; his box office hits like *Fast and Furious, San Andreas, Central Intelligence,* and *Moana* have earned billions of dollars. But he calls his production company Seven Bucks Productions because it's a humble reminder that life wasn't always this way.

Back in 1995, Johnson was in and out of depression because of his career. He had been playing football in the Canadian Football League but was cut two months into the season. He was sitting in his pickup truck with only seven dollars in his pocket: "In 1995, I had seven bucks in my pocket and knew two things: I was broke as hell and one day I wouldn't be." It was the turning point in his life because he began to prepare for what he had been praying for.

He decided to follow his father and grandfather and go into wrestling. He started wrestling under the name Rocky, but after a few bouts, the fans rejected him. Undeterred, he decided to change his stage name to "The Rock," and this adjustment, along with a work ethic that few people on the planet possess, proved to be the foundation that would transform him into one of the biggest entertainers in the world.

It's time to start doing your part no matter what circumstances you face.

STUDY TO SHOW YOURSELF APPROVED

Prayer can open your mind, but it can't fill it completely. If you want to be in the fullness of God's purpose, you need to study more. The great author and motivational speaker Jim Rohn said, "If you want to be healthy study health . . . if you want to be wealthy, study wealth . . . if you want to be happy, study happiness." I agree completely. If you want to be successful in your field, study. There are knowledge and understanding that are vital to your success that you cannot attain no matter how long or fervently you pray.

No matter how much I prayed, prayer couldn't teach me how to be a successful executive. That only came with intense study of the industry and lots of experience. From there, I was able to move on to other passions: author, TV personality, producer. None of these things would have happened if I hadn't taken the time to study my industry, learn trends, learn how to develop scripts, figure out how to navigate personalities, learn what makes a project commercially viable, and so on.

In order to be successful, engage in intense, consistent study of the field in which you want to excel. Read. Assist more experienced people. Watch skilled professionals at work and take note of everything they do. If you don't understand why they did something, ask. You'd be surprised at how willing most people will be to give you a response to well thought-out and insightful questions.

Jesus knew all this. He absolutely took time to pray. But he was also on the move. There were towns that were not receptive to his message, so he would move on. He was looking for people he could inspire but also people who could help him prepare. He would go to the synagogue to listen and learn and preach. He knew that his time of impact would come when he was thirty years old, and every moment before that was for preparation and study. He had to learn the politics of the region, the economics of the region, and the religion of the region so that when his time came, he would be effective. Without question, he spent time in prayer, but he spent *more* time learning and practicing.

I meet many people who say they want to work in Hollywood, but their lack of study betrays the passion they say they have. If I ask them to tell me what they liked about the last movie they watched, and they talk about a movie that came out a year ago, I know they're not taking their would-be career seriously. It's like talking to someone who says he wants to be a sportscaster but hasn't watched a game since the 2015 Super Bowl. If someone is truly passionate about an entertainment career, I can tell by the questions they ask me and their response to my answers. Both tell me if they've done their homework. If they haven't, I know they're not ready.

**How you study your industry will either support
or betray what you say you're passionate about.**

If you want to reach the next level in your career, become a student not just of where you are today but also of where you aspire to be in the future. Begin to study and put yourself in environments conducive to where you want to go. For example, if your dream is to start your own software company, learning about programming and even getting a computer science degree are both important, but they're not enough. You have to do as Jesus did and put yourself in environments that will change who you are. Attend coding competitions like Google Code Jam. Go to startup events and boot camps near you. Go to the Consumer Electronics Show. Ask questions, listen, meet people, and learn what you can't from prayer alone.

Away from the Workplace

This approach to prayer can benefit you in other areas of your life. For example, in something I've already talked about—physical fitness and health—God won't make you lean and ripped, but He can give you the discipline and strength of will to stick to a workout and diet program when the going gets tough. If you have fitness goals, pray about them and make sure they're the right goals. Then hit the gym hard and show the equipment no mercy. Stay focused and put in the work and you'll see results in time.

IF PRAYER ISN'T ENOUGH, WHEN IS IT NECESSARY?

As I said in the beginning, this book is about applying spiritual and secular principles to achieve spiritual and secular success. I've been very clear that in going after your goals, there is no substitute for learning, work, and persistence. But doesn't prayer also play a role in positioning you for the life you want?

Of course, it does. It's critical—to a healthy soul but also to finding success. These are some scenarios in which prayer can give you an important edge:

- **You're uncertain about your purpose.** Here, prayer is essential. If you don't know what your purpose is or what career you should pursue, and you fear wasting years on a direction that will prove unfulfilling, ask God to reveal His purpose for your life, as He did for me. Look at your talents and gifts. Keep in mind that He may reveal your purpose not directly but subtly. You might feel a strong pull toward one industry or type of work or meet someone who's engaged in a career that you hadn't thought about but, upon further investigation, find fascinating. Whatever the process, discovering your God-ordained purpose is an unsurpassed blessing, a direct and meaningful connection to your divine destiny.

• **You're being asked to compromise your values.** As I've mentioned, I observe the Sabbath, from sunset Friday to sunset Saturday. I don't do any office work and spend my time in study, prayer, and fellowship with my church community and immediate family. But more than once I have faced pressure to bend my Sabbath observation—to attend a screening, read scripts, or go to work meetings. When the pressures of work make us question our convictions, prayer is invaluable. It centers us and reminds us of what is really important. Prayer can give us the wisdom and fortitude to stand firm and handle difficult situations.

Every time I've been asked to waive my Sabbath observance for work, I pray and then stand firm on my conviction, refusing to bow to pressure or compromise. Ironically, these refusals have actually helped my career, not hurt it. You'll face similar situations, and when you do, pray and ask for guidance on how to handle the situation. What I know is that, even if people don't agree with you, when you stay true to your convictions (no matter the cost), you will earn yourself respect from those around you.

Look at Desmond Doss in the movie *Hacksaw Ridge,* based on a true story. Doss was an army medic in World War II, yet he would not use a weapon because he believed it was wrong to kill. He faced ridicule, abuse, and tremendous pressure to compromise, but he resisted. As a result, he saved many lives and made history.

- **You face a crossroads in your career.** Being offered a new position? Faced with the chance to go back to school for an advanced degree? Unsure of what to do? Prayer can help bring clarity to the situation and help you make the right decision.

- **You're facing a steep uphill climb.** Maybe you've been handed a difficult, tedious, but important project. Maybe you've started at a new company, and things aren't going as planned. You know that hard work and persistence are the keys to advancement, but that doesn't make them any easier. So, ask God for strength in daily prayer—in fact, pray every time you find your will faltering. After all, Isaiah 40:31 (NIV) says, "Those who hope in the LORD will renew their strength. They will soar on wings like eagles; they will run and not grow weary, they will walk and not be faint."

HOW TO PRAY

Prayer is communication. Prayer is connection. The more you pray, the more you become aligned with God and have a better relationship with Him. First, you will begin to better understand who you are. Second, you will have more peace. Third, you will have more power because you will be in communion with the One who created you. Those are the reasons for prayer.

The Bible assures us that God will give you your heart's desire if you ask in the name of Jesus. God does not expect us to just believe in Him. He understands that He created us in the flesh, and our flesh needs reassurance and reaffirmation of His existence and power. God is always a God of demonstration. He will demonstrate who He is and will reward those who believe in Him, as He did from Moses all the way to Paul and Peter.

God does not hold it against us that we ask Him for things. But if we only relegate our prayer life to asking for things, we will never understand everything that prayer can do. Prayer is about the relationship, the connection, and the alignment. When I get up from praying, I feel like I'm connected, have a greater understanding of my life, and am aligned with fulfilling my purpose. Then I have to go into the field and get the job done. Some answers to prayers don't even happen until you're taking action.

Sometimes, an answer to a prayer will come in the moment while you're doing the job. You'll be in a meeting and think, "This person just said something that was an answer to my prayer. God, this is fascinating. Here I am on the job, and look what You're doing."

These are some other tips for practical prayer that help your life goals:

- **Pray from a place of humility.** You understand that God is all-powerful. You understand that you come to God humble, grateful for life, grateful for the opportunity to communicate, grateful for the opportunity to come before Him. Humility is a big part of praying.

- **Don't immediately get into, "Lord, this is what I want."** It's more about cleansing. Is there excessive ego in you? Is there negativity in you? Say, "I want to be the best person I can be, so whatever is not aligned with that, Lord, take that away. Show me what needs work. How can I be more effective in serving You?"

- **Pray every day when you get up.** Before you check Facebook, Twitter, Instagram, or email, have you checked in with God? We tend to be more concerned with our social media connections than we really are with God. We are addicted to our phones and what others are doing as well as other people's perceptions of us, and we want to make sure we're staying connected and don't miss anything. But what if we're missing what God has for us? In order to have a successful day, you have to get plugged in with who God wants you to be today.

- **End the day with prayer.** Thanking God for what He did during the day, clearing your mind of what you didn't get done, and preparing yourself for what's going to happen tomorrow will produce tremendous change in your life.

- **During the day, pray as needed.** If prayer is a conversation, we should be engaging in that conversation throughout the day. For example, I pray before big meetings—even while I'm in meetings—that God will tell me the right things to say. I pray before speaking engagements. I pray before television appearances. I incorporate prayer into my entire day, asking God for courage, wisdom, eloquence, or insight.

- **Finally, after you pray, become a beast.** Humility ends when you get off your knees. Get out there and go to war to fulfill your purpose and pursue excellence while you do. Say, "God has great things in mind for me, and He's put me in this job. Whom do I need to call today? What connections do I need to make? How do I become better at the job I'm doing?" Go after your goal in a way that is focused and controlled but ambitious and aggressive. Don't allow yourself to live at a standard that's less than you're capable of.

In the morning after I pray, I go to the gym, come home,

switch clothes, go to the office, figure out whom I need to call, which emails I need to return, review my schedule for the day, and make sure I have what I need so I'm prepared for my meetings. I have a plan and put it into action. Instead of letting the day happen to you, happen to the day!

If all you've got is yourself, your job, and your relationship with God, you've got enough. The question is, what are you going to do with it?

THOU SHALT

» Develop a daily prayer practice and stick with it no matter what.
» Prepare and study. Learn everything you can about the business you're in—or the one you want to be in. Learn the people, the trends, the technology, everything. Become an expert.
» Find mentors and other resources to learn everything you can about the work you do today and the work you want to be doing.
» Remember that if you give everything you have to reach your goals, God will manifest them when the time is right.

THOU SHALT NOT

» Lose your intensity or desire.
» Allow any career pressure to dissuade you from God's purpose, even if others think your goals are unrealistic.
» Pray to God for things that you don't need His help to do.

2 | YOU ARE THE TALENT

Your talent is God's gift to you.
What you do with it is your gift back to God.
—Leo Buscaglia

Everyone has talent, and church was the incubator for mine. Church was the place where I began to speak and harness my ability to communicate in public. When I was fifteen years old, we were having Youth Day at Wings of Love, and out of the blue, I was asked to speak. My older brother had been the speaker the year before, but I had never preached before. I had run for the student body president at school, and that was about it. But I said I'd try.

The sermon went very well, and after I finished, everyone told me, "You should go into ministry. You should become a pastor."

But even at fifteen, I knew what my calling was. "No," I said. "My goal is to be in Hollywood. I want to work on films, I want to work in television, and I want to be a part of entertainment." Nobody understood. Because they could see I had the gift of preaching, they thought that my desire to go to Hollywood was a rebuke of my spiritual gift.

I wish people would have said to me, "DeVon, you can be whoever you want to be, so keep praying, keep working, and let God determine where your gifts will take you." But that type of encouragement was rare. As a result, when I started my career in Hollywood years later, I didn't think of myself as someone who had talent. At that time, I only thought of myself as someone who would be fortunate if I got the opportunity to service those who had the real talent.

Most people I knew didn't believe that my desired career path was the "right" one. Most didn't see how it would lead me closer to God. As they saw it, there is a wall between the sacred and the secular. Many people still believe to this day that Hollywood is not the place for a person of faith. While growing up and even today, I fight those views so I can pursue what I believe God wants me to do.

This chapter's Commandment is that you are not just a vessel for talent:

You Are the Talent

God gifts us each with unique talents and calls us to use them to fulfill some part of His purpose. Remember what Paul said in Romans 12:6–8 (NIV): "We have different gifts, according to the grace given to each of us. If your gift is prophesying, then prophesy in accordance with your faith; if it is serving, then serve; if it is teaching, then teach; if it is to encourage, then give encouragement; if it is giving, then give generously; if it is to lead, do it diligently; if it is to show mercy, do it cheerfully."

Paul was right. We've all been gifted with a variety of unique skills and talents. But talent is more than just a set of skills. It's who we are—who *you* are. You are an agent of change, a force for good in the world. Looking at talent this way means your value in the eyes of God and man is about more than what you do—it's about who you are. Let's take a closer look at this idea.

DEFINITION OF TALENT 1.0

The common definition of the word *talent* is an ability in which someone shows unusual proficiency. People can have talent in almost anything, from singing and cooking to shooting three-pointers or fixing cars. Talent is the most important commodity in any field. It's what employers pay for and sports franchises draft for. In Hollywood, talent is currency. It doesn't guarantee you a career, because hard work and so many other factors go into success apart from natural ability. But if you believe you are uniquely talented, you have a big advantage over the competition, which is fierce.

Because for years I didn't think of myself as possessing talent, it took me a long time to realize that I actually did. I had a real talent for communicating, motivating, and inspiring people, not just through making movies and TV shows but through preaching and speaking. When I saw this, I said, "This is what will set me apart. This is the foundation of my life, and I'd better start using it intentionally so I can harness the thing that makes me distinctive and propels my success."

My true talent is as a *coach*. I coach people into spiritual success. I exist to motivate people with the urge, information, or ability to do something positive in their lives by creating a feeling of hope. Because if you don't have hope, nothing else happens. Whether it's a book, a movie, a television appearance, or a social media post, everything I do is knit together by that mission statement. Humbly, and by the grace of God, I point their hope in a direction that helps them begin to make the changes that success requires. That's the talent that defines me—to cut through the noise, be a sympathetic, empathetic voice, and have the information to help someone, no matter where they may be in their life.

I believe that's what made me stand out as an executive. That's what helped me create a business inside Sony. That's what gave me the platform to start my own company. That's what gave me the platform to write my first book. That's what got me on *Oprah's Super Soul Sunday*. That's what allows me to travel around the world and speak. That's what got me on *The Dr. Oz Show*. The same gift I discovered at fifteen is flourishing now that I'm thirty-eight, in ways that no one could have imagined. Why? Because I recognized that God did not just gift me with a talent but with an even greater revelation: I *am* talent . . . and you are, too.

However, there's a second definition of talent that's even more important. Yes, talent is what you can do. But talent is also *who you are*.

DEFINITION OF TALENT 2.0

Embracing the idea that you are talent means you must embrace the fact that you have star power. The dictionary defines a star as an outstandingly talented performer, and while people around the world are obsessed with Hollywood stars, their obsession often obscures the star that lies within themselves. As a Christian, I believe and acknowledge that Jesus is the star of my life, but this does not negate the fact that we are all fearfully and wonderfully made for a divine purpose. We have to walk in the confidence of this revelation in order to succeed.

In Hollywood, *talent* is what we call the people who drive the industry as a whole. Hollywood is an industry driven by content. So, "the talent" are the ones that create the content (writers, directors, producers, and certain agents) or bring the content to life (actors, musicians). In the business, when we talk about those people in shorthand, they are referred to as "the talent." Who they are, not what they do. Without them harnessing their abilities in unique and dynamic ways, there is no Hollywood. They are talent. And whether you realize it or not, so are you.

I believe that God sees each one of us as "the talent," which not only means having a special gift but also having the desire to develop and use it. For example, God might gift one person with the talent of playing a musical instrument and the passion to be a professional musician while gifting someone else not only with the talent to train dogs but also with a deep love of them. In every case, he wants to nurture those talents. But why don't we hear this more? Why aren't our pastors and leaders in our churches helping us more often to recognize our talent and to nurture it?

Growing up in the church I found that certain talents and gifts were anointed, ones that could be used within the church, or for a directly Christian purpose, like singing, playing music, or preaching. If you can play, sing, preach, or teach a good Bible study or children's program, others will smile upon your talent.

But what about the gifts that don't fit into the often narrow definition of what a Christian should be doing? I've seen people discouraged or put into a box or even ridiculed. There are infinite ways to serve God, and God has given out a multitude of gifts that don't always fit within the confines of what is traditionally accepted within the church. Within the church, some expressions of talent make people uncomfortable (because they go against the norm) about encouraging others to develop their true talents.

More often than not, the leaders in our churches want the people in their congregations to live by following the example set for them by Jesus. That's admirable, but sometimes they miss the mark because they forget who Jesus really was. He wasn't a conformist. He was radically talented and spent his adult life exercising his gifts and talents in ways that the church leaders of his time disagreed with. As I mentioned in the previous chapter, Jesus spent years learning about the political and social fabric of the world in which he lived and in many ways disrupting that fabric with the power of his message and his talent. To truly live like Jesus means to be a bold, out-of-the-box thinker—a voracious disrupter of societal norms that go against the fullness of who God created you to be.

(This is another time when prayer becomes important. When you talk to God about what he has called you to do and how he has gifted you, you can know that you are moving forward anointed, even if those around you disagree.)

In entertainment, talent is *everything*. If you are an extraordinary talent, and you have developed your gifts to a professional level, doors open for you. Yes, it's important to have a good agent and team, but the talent is the team leader and necessary for the team to win. The thing is, it's not just that way in the movie and television business but in every business. If you are talented at attending to the needs of others, eventually you might be called to go into the customer service field, and one day that might lead to running a successful company. If you are talented at managing people, eventually you might be called to become an executive at a major corporation and one day, perhaps even start your own company. If you're such a gifted baker that your pies leave people speechless, a world of opportunity is open to you, from pastry chef at a fine restaurant to your own bakery.

Talent is the bottom line. Talent reshapes the world, shows us new things we couldn't have imagined, and inspires us to live boldly and joyously. But people of faith—and the churches that help shape us—often badly misunderstand the nature of talent. We fail to grasp these four key ideas:

1. **You can recycle the box that people try to put you in.** People are often uncomfortable around great talent. It may make them self-conscious that they haven't found or developed their own talent, they might be afraid of what they don't understand, they could fear that pursuing one's true calling as a career means winding up broke and miserable, or maybe a combination of all three. Whatever the reason, I know from my own experience that people will often try to put your talent into a box—to confine it, limit it, and shape it into something they can make sense of.

   Here's the truth: the church can teach and equip you, but there's a limit to what the church can do for you as it relates to your God-given gift. If you've been called to pursue a career outside the church, then it's especially important to put yourself in secular environments where you can begin to incubate your talent—discover its levers, boundaries, and potential.

   Recycling the box means throwing away the box that others try to put you in. It is not your responsibility to make other people comfortable with your talent. If they want to put your talent in a box out of fear or discomfort, that's their problem, not yours. As people of faith, we toss aside those boxes with integrity and honor and remember it's the people who won't let their gifts be tamed or discouraged who change the world.

2. **You need a talent mentality.** When I say that everyone is a talent, I mean that everyone has been gifted by God with a *consequential* ability—a gift that, when used properly, makes a difference in the world. That's important to remember because church teachings can sometimes be misinterpreted into living a life of passivity—just sitting back and waiting for God to make important things happen in our lives. But if that were true, why would he have made us talent and gifted us with unique abilities if he didn't expect us to play an active role in our own talent development?

God made you talent so you could be confident in your gift and what you can do. The scope of that gift doesn't matter; what you do with it does. You must have a *talent mentality*. It all starts in the mind with your belief in who you were created to be. Let's say you're a teacher. If you inspire students to love learning, it doesn't matter if you impact one student a year or ten thousand. Your belief that you are talent will change not only your life but the lives of everyone you come in contact with.

Having a *talent mentality* means that you project a confidence based on knowing who you are and what you have to offer. I have seen people with limited experience excel above those with more experience because they possessed this talent mentality, and the more experienced people did not. Confidence is a fragrance everyone wants to smell. When you feel good about who you are, and you know what you can do and you own it, you position yourself to become unstoppable.

David had a talent mentality before he ever became king. Before he fought Goliath, he projected a confidence and an authority that was essential to his success. He was the only one in the kingdom of Israel brave enough to face the giant.

All he had was a slingshot and five stones, yet he didn't have a "slingshot-and-five-stones" mentality. He proclaimed to Goliath,

> You come against me with sword and spear and javelin, but I come against you in the name of the Lord Almighty, the god of the armies of Israel, whom you have defied. This day the Lord will hand you over to me, and I'll strike you down and cut off your head. Today I will give the carcasses of the Philistine army to the birds of the air and the beasts of the earth, and the whole world will know that there is a God in Israel. All those gathered here will know that it is not by sword or spear that the Lord saves, for the battle is the Lord's, and he will give all of you into our hands!" (1 Samuel 17:45–17, NIV)

Doesn't this get you hyped!? What would happen if all of us projected this level of confidence even before we were certain of the outcome!? It was this mentality that contributed to his eventual defeat of Goliath because he thought like a giant slayer even before he became one!

If you take nothing else from this chapter, know that even if you don't see or feel it right now, God made you an extraordinary, consequential, important talent destined to do great and life-changing things.

3. **You either are talent or you service talent.** Talent calls the shots in Hollywood. It's the ultimate arbiter of opportunity. Talent creates opportunities and opens doors. The entertainment industry is divided into two categories: those who are talent and those who service talent. *Period.* However, this isn't limited to

Hollywood; in any profession, those who run the company or the division heads are considered the talent while those who work for them are servicing their talent. No matter your field, you must recognize the value of what you do, who you are, and who you really aspire to be. Are you content with servicing talent the rest of your life? Or are you determined to *become* the talent?

Let me be clear: even if your life's calling is to service others' talent, *if you never come into a talent mentality, you may service talent for the rest of your life without ever claiming the talent within you.* That would be tragic.

4. **You can serve talent and be talent at the same time.** This might seem to contradict what I just wrote, but if you have a talent mentality, it doesn't. Suppose you're working at Google as a software developer. You could have incredible programming and development talents, and you know that they make you unique and valuable. But at the same time, you're low on the ladder. To get anywhere, you have to serve people. But because you have a talent mentality, you don't chafe at serving. You know that the only way to learn, achieve mastery, and get opportunities to advance is to do your apprenticeship, learn, and climb up through the organization. So, you most certainly can serve talent and be talent at the same time.

God puts you in positions not to frustrate you but to give you the opportunity to hone your talent. This is an important spiritual principle to apply in the secular world. To be both servant and master is to be like Jesus, who was both humble healer and teacher and the bold, politically savvy, warrior-like Son of God. We can be these two things at the same time.

False Idols

Sometimes we wish with all our hearts that we had talent in an area where we just don't have it. God has given each of us talent, but maybe you're pursuing an area that He has not ordained for you. The key to understanding the difference is to seek confirmation of your gift over a period of time. Try what you believe you're supposed to do, but be open to the feedback you get from professionals and be careful not to delude yourself into thinking that you're good at something if you've gotten feedback to the contrary. Better to have a little disappointment that clears the way for what God really wants you to do than to waste your life chasing something you were never meant to do.

YOU ARE A VALUE CREATOR

None of us live on an island. We depend on each other for support, help, and the services we need. Since you're talent, you have the ability to create value. The greater the value you create, and the fewer people who can do what you can do, the greater compensation you will receive. That's why superstar professional athletes like Clayton Kershaw and LeBron James make salaries of more than $30 million per year: they attract huge numbers of fans for their teams, and they can do things that few other human beings on the planet can do.

Talent is about value creation.

However, it's vitally important that you not allow yourself to be blinded by the entertainment and sports paradigms of talent. Yes, great rappers, singers, actors, and athletes are wildly gifted talents and might be compensated for their abilities at levels greater than most people will ever see. But almost any gift, no matter the size, can create value.

At the churches across the country where I have spoken, I have heard musicians—singers, choirs, and instrumentalists—who made my spirit soar or, alternately, made me weep with their gifts. For the most part, these were not people who were playing on a big stage. They weren't playing to a concert stadium or to a megachurch crowd of thousands of ecstatic worshippers. They were playing for just a few people, yet their gift was powerful and palpable. It didn't matter that the audience was small; in those moments of transcendent music, God was singing and playing through them. You could feel the Holy Spirit fill the space. It was amazing. Talk about intensity and impact! Their gifts were creating incredible value for everyone who heard them, and it didn't matter that they didn't have songs for sale on iTunes. Talents can be *anything*. Value can come from *anywhere*.

If your customer service skills keep a retail business running smoothly and profitably, you're creating value, and you are a talent.

If your experience as a contractor helps people keep their homes in great repair and earns you a six-month backlog of referrals, you're creating value, and you are a talent.

If you're a home healthcare worker who helps elderly individuals remain in their homes so they can enjoy their independence and families as long as possible, you're creating value, and you are a talent.

If you're the Uber driver who's decorated his vehicle, knows every great hole-in-the-wall restaurant in your city, and has such a great sense of humor that passengers specifically request rides with you even when they have to wait, you're creating value, and you are a talent.

Talent is what creates value for others. It's that simple. These are some other ways to know if what you're pursuing is truly a talent from God:

1. **You love doing it.** Do you hate numbers and accounting and wonder how in the world anyone could do that boring, repetitive work and not lose their minds? I completely understand. But there are some people who love figures and bookkeeping and profit and loss statements and would rather be working with them than doing whatever you're doing. If you love what you do, even if you don't get paid for it, it's likely to be a talent. God places that love in our hearts because He knows that the more we love what He asks us to do, the more likely we are to do it and to excel at it.

2. **It stretches you.** God isn't interested in your comfort zone if it doesn't serve Him. His gift to you is His gift whether you're comfortable with it or not—but if you're not, that's a great sign that it is something that makes you talent. If nurturing this God-given ability pushes you to test yourself or leads you down career paths that you're not completely comfortable with, embrace it. God wants us all to stretch and grow beyond what we believe we can do today and to turn that slight current of fear into exultation.

3. **It validates you.** If what you're spending your time doing, whether it's your career or currently just a hobby, makes you feel like your days have meaning and that you're adding something important to the world, that's important validation. Even if only you and God see that it's meaningful, that's enough.

There's nobility, even divinity, in humble, simple work done well and with dignity.

Exodus

If you've been doing exemplary work year after year at your workplace, and new opportunities still aren't coming your way, it might be time to move on. Value yourself and your talent highly, and at the right time, ask for the opportunities you've earned. If your boss isn't listening, don't be afraid to head for the door. If nothing else, it's a terrific negotiating tactic.

NO DISCIPLINE, NO DESTINY

Three-time heavyweight boxing champion Muhammad Ali, commonly referred to as "The Greatest of All Time," didn't earn that moniker because of what he did in the ring. He earned it because of how he trained. Ali was famously quoted as saying, "I hated every minute of training, but I said, 'Don't quit. Suffer now and live the rest of your life as a champion.'" He also said, "The fight is won or lost far away from witnesses—behind the lines, in the gym, and out there on the road, long before I dance under those lights."

Angelo Dundee, Ali's trainer, told *Muscle & Performance* magazine, "I never had to ask him to come to the gym . . . He was there before I even got there . . . He was always first in and last to leave. He'd even come to train when he wasn't fighting." Greatness can only show up in the ring of life when you've practiced greatness outside the ring of life. Do an assessment of your discipline and look for areas where you are not as disciplined as you need to be, and then make adjustments immediately. What if your prayers for career advancement have already been answered but they have not manifested because you aren't displaying the discipline required to handle the opportunity?

Stephen King once wrote, "Talent is cheaper than table salt. What separates the talented individual from the successful one is a lot of hard work." As you either begin to determine what your talent is or, having identified the way in which you are talent, try to develop your talent into a lifelong career path, remember this:

Talent alone is never enough.

In the last chapter, I encouraged you to make this your motto: Pray and Prepare. When it comes to using your talent, study and preparation are just as important as God-given ability. There is no amount of raw talent, no matter how prodigious or historically great, that will vault you to the top of whatever profession you choose. You're a naturally God-gifted surgeon? That's wonderful, but you'll never get a license or be allowed to bring a scalpel near a patient unless you graduate from medical school. You're brilliant at the piano? Congratulations. However, if you wish to play Lincoln Center, you'll need years and years of lessons and practice. It's the same with any profession.

From a young age, I had a natural talent for speaking and teaching and an intense passion for working in Hollywood. But just because I had talent and passion for something didn't mean I knew how to do it! I spent years refining every aspect of my gifts. I spoke and preached in many churches, first up and down California and then all around the U.S. I went to college and used my internship to absorb every bit of knowledge I could.

I studied great preachers and motivational speakers. I also took classes to understand the Bible better so I could prepare more dynamic messages. I immersed myself in the entertainment industry, learned how the business worked, and dug into information about marketing and publicity. I've spent hundreds of hours reading scripts and spent many hours more on movie sets watching directors, cinematographers, lighting designers, sound recorders, stunt doubles, and dozens of other movie professionals ply their trade. In other words, knowing that I had talent drove me to learn and work nonstop to develop that talent to its fullest potential: *mastery*.

If you want a career that lasts for decades, brings you financial rewards, and fills your spirit with the joy of God's purpose, strive for mastery. I'm not there myself yet; I might never get there . . . and it doesn't matter. It's the pursuit of mastery, not its achievement, that is important. Mastery is when you become preeminent in your field. For example, most people struggle to play decent chords on the guitar, but there are a few who can pick up the instrument and make it sing with ease. That ease is an illusion; they have talent, of course, but the reason their playing is so flawless is because of all the effort that went into endless practice. That's what it takes to reach mastery.

Wherever you are in developing your talent, be prepared with the discipline needed to harness your gift. Discipline—the will and persistence to work and practice every day—is the key to unlocking your destiny. Have the discipline to walk the path set down for you by God and try not to veer away from it. There's no substitute for this. Also, don't let yourself be seduced into laziness by your talent. If you're really gifted in something, it can be easy to take shortcuts and skimp on the work, study, and preparation. But that's a trap.

Here's why. Let's say you're a young lawyer, and when it comes to drafting legal briefs, you are pure superstar talent. But while you have a once-in-a-generation talent for legal writing, you're lazy about studying case law. You rely on the work of other lawyers in writing your briefs and coast on your raw ability. But as your work keeps getting results, your firm throws you more and more responsibility. You try to bluff your way with raw talent, but your lack of study of the law starts to show. Finally, you're named the lead lawyer on a big case and, since you're unprepared to handle the responsibility, the likelihood is that you'll blow it.

You are talent, but you're not necessarily *prepared—yet.* That comes when you mix talent with hard work and discipline. Do not let your ability make you complacent.

TALENT IS ON LOAN; STAY HUMBLE

For perspective, read what Paul wrote in the first part of the verse from Romans 12:3–5 (NIV): "For by the grace given me I say to every one of you: Do not think of yourself more highly than you ought, but rather think of yourself with sober judgment, in accordance with the faith God has distributed to each of you. For just as each of us has one body with many members, and these members do not all have the same function, so in Christ we, though many, form one body, and each member belongs to all the others."

At the time he wrote his famous letters to the Romans, Paul was about to leave for Jerusalem to aid poor Christians and then head for Rome where he hoped to gain support for a mission to Spain. He knew the journey to Rome, where Christians were few and persecuted, might be hazardous. But in his letter, he isn't concerned with the dangers. Instead, he encourages Roman believers not only to embrace their gifts but to remember that they come from God, Who wants them to use their gifts wisely and well.

Paul's letter is a beautiful example of a vital principle surrounding talent, that it is not ours. Talent is only on loan from the Lord. It's important not to let even great talent lead to arrogance or the presumption that because you have it, you don't need God. As great UCLA basketball coach John Wooden once said, "Talent is God given. Be humble. Fame is man-given. Be grateful. Conceit is self-given. Be careful."

It's important to remember why you have this gift: to serve God and fulfill the destiny for which He has chosen you. Humility should always accompany talent. The word *humility* means "to go low." To experience the power of God, you must go under his mighty hand. He didn't say, "Stand on my hand, and I will prop you up"; He said, "I will put my hand over you." God did not grant you talent for your purposes, but for His.

Part of humility is admitting, "I'm not where I want to be in my career." In our social media–driven culture, that's not something you might like to admit. Maybe you'd rather fake it. You present a public image that says, "I'm doing exactly what I want to be doing," but the reality is that you're not. If you have great talent, perhaps you feel even worse: "How can I *not* have the career I want—the life I want—when I have this talent?"

There are many reasons. God's appointed time for your rise may not have come yet. You may not have put in enough work. Or maybe you've been proud and forgotten what your talent is for. Remember, God opposes the proud and shows favor to the humble. We often look at humility as being the opposite of strength, but it's not. Many of the most influential and powerful people in the world are also the humblest. They recognize that this not about them; it's about what God does *through* them. As a result, they are blessed.

Away from the Workplace

When you're just starting out in a career, you don't want to be patient. You know you're going to be at the bottom of the flowchart, and it stinks. How will anybody know what you can do if you can't show them? I get it. Know what I did? I kept my mouth shut and worked harder. I knew I had to prove myself, so I went about it. That's good advice in any career. Pay your dues. Keep your mouth closed and your ears open. Read. Learn. Listen. Eventually, you'll get a chance to show your talent—and you'll be ready.

HOW TO MAKE THE MOST OF YOUR TALENT

With hard work, humility, and practice, you can achieve mastery in your talent. But it isn't that easy. If it were, then more people would be enjoying fulfilling, prosperous lives. They're not. Too many people, even if they've found the courage to take their talent out of its box, still struggle to stay the course and endure until success happens. If you're frustrated in your work, if you feel like you're going nowhere, here are some things to try:

- **Become indispensable.** As talent, you might have an ability no-body else possesses, but that doesn't make you indispensable. Doing things no one else can is called *applied talent,* and that will make you impossible to replace or live without. Later in this book, we'll devote a whole chapter to this idea when we explore the Commandment *Your Difference Is Your Destiny,* but for now the key question is, what can you do to create value in a way nobody else can? My key to indispensability has been my faith background, which gives me a unique perspective on different types of projects that other filmmakers weren't making. It gives me insight on different strategies for reaching people of faith. This has helped me stand out among other executives, and now it helps me stand out among other producers because I understand the faith-based audience in a way that they don't. I can do something they can't. Use your talent to discover what you can do in a way others can't, and you will become indispensable.

- **Use "virtual mentors."** Make a list of the leaders in your field. Now, in some instances, if you reach out to these leaders, they might respond, and that would be an ideal way to try and attain their mentorship. However, we become frustrated if we can't reach the people we most admire because their schedules are too busy. But you can still get that person as a mentor, even if you never meet them. Study their careers, follow their social media posts, research the projects they are working on—you can learn a tremendous amount about how to navigate your career by studying theirs. I wish I had the time to personally mentor all the people who come to me, but I don't have the capacity. That's why I write books and speak—so, even if you never meet me, you still can have a way to find the knowledge you seek. Make a list of your virtual mentors ASAP, and start immersing yourself in what they are doing.

- **Most important of all, never forget that your talent comes from God.** Remain open in your spirit to His guidance. He will show you new ways to use your gifts, new areas in which you can apply them. If you're listening, He'll correct you if you let ego take you off course (although the correction might be a little unpleasant). Pay attention for those signs that it's time to transition, to take your talent in a new direction or to a new organization. Remember, your talent is on loan from Heaven. Invest it wisely.

Thou Shalt

» Pray for humility.
» Try to help your church nurture talent beyond the pulpit.
» Network to find new constituents.
» Pursue virtual mentors.
» Recognize and live in the confidence that you ARE talent.

Thou Shalt Not

» Let anyone put your talent in a box.
» Phone it in.
» Envy those with greater talents.

3

YOU HAVE TO CARRY A CROWN BEFORE YOU CAN WEAR ONE

> You are not here merely to make a living. You are here in order to
> enable the world to live more amply, with greater vision, with a
> finer spirit of hope and achievement. You are here to enrich the
> world, and you impoverish yourself if you forget the errand.
> —Woodrow Wilson

In the summer before my junior year of high school, I ended up working for a nonprofit organization in downtown Oakland called OCCUR (Oakland Citizens Committee for Urban Renewal). My aunt Sondra Alexander ran the nonprofit along with the executive director, David Glover. David went to Howard University and was roommates with Takashi Bufford, who at that time had written and produced the box office hits *Set It Off* and *Booty Call*. I wanted to learn from others in the industry I wanted to be in, so I asked David if he could arrange a meeting between me and Takashi, and he did. Takashi was terrific. He encouraged me to become a screenwriter, but I told him I didn't feel like that was my calling. Then he said, "If I were you, I would try and get an internship with Handprint."

At that time, Handprint Entertainment—run by Benny Medina, Jeff Pollack, and James Lassiter—was one of the hottest management and production companies in the business. Their clients were some of the biggest names in entertainment, including Will Smith, Jada Pinkett Smith, Babyface, Sean "P. Diddy" Combs, and Jennifer Lopez. Benny Medina is one of the most successful managers in all of entertainment, a legend who helped transform the careers of Babyface, J-Lo, Mariah Carey, and many others. He was also notorious for having high standards (code for "difficult"). I put in my resume with Jeru Tillman, Benny's assistant, and a few weeks later I got a call to come in for an interview.

I interviewed with Dale Ottley, the general manager, but we didn't get off to a great start. The moment I walked in, Dale held up my resume and said, "Look." I had put my head shot on my resume, thinking I was being cool (a real facepalm moment), but she had drawn an "X" through my picture. She said, "This isn't a modeling agency. There are some people who won't hire you just because of how you look." Whoa. I was eighteen and thought I knew what was what, and I was getting an education!

However, we rebounded from that when she asked, "Why do you want to be in entertainment?"

I said, "I want to be in entertainment because I want to make change."

Her eyebrows went up. "You want to make money?" It was a funny miscommunication that I quickly corrected.

"No. Well, I mean, there's nothing wrong with making money. But I'm not talking about that kind of change. I'm talking about making change in the world. Entertainment is one of the most powerful industries in the world, and if I can be a part of it and actually make content, I think I can bring change to people's lives in a positive way."

Dale really liked that, and we had a good conversation. Then she said, "Is there anything else you want me to know?" And I heard God speaking to me: *Tell her about the Sabbath.*

In my spirit, I replied, *No, I'll tell her about the Sabbath after I get the internship.*

He insisted: *DeVon, tell her about the Sabbath. Trust me.* I took a deep breath and said, "There is one more thing. I observe the Sabbath from Friday night sundown to Saturday night sundown, and if taking this job requires me to work on the Sabbath, then I'm not going to take it."

She paused, and I think my heart stopped for a second. I thought, *Lord, why did you do this to me? I'm trying to get my foot in the door, and now it's about to close.* Then Dale said, "No worries. We can work around that." That internship was the key that unlocked the door to my entire career. It also introduced me to the next Commandment:

You Have to Carry a Crown Before You Can Wear One

Before you can lead, you have to serve. God has an extraordinary destiny in mind for you, as He does for all of us. You might have been told that you will do great things, and I have no doubt that you will. But both God and man have a learning curve. God will never bring you an opportunity before you're ready to make the most of it, and the career world demands that you prove yourself. The idea is simple: having a great purpose doesn't mean you're ready to fulfill it today, and there is much we can learn while we're working in that direction. I would discover this firsthand while I was working at Handprint.

DRIVING MR. MEDINA

On my first day working at Handprint, they didn't have anything for me to do. My "office" was a sort of kitchen/file room without a comfortable place to sit, and I just hung out there with no instruction but constantly afraid of doing something I had not been asked to do.

But as the hours passed, I thought, *I have my foot in the door. The onus is on me to make something of this. What am I going to do?* I started doing the only thing I knew how to do: *serve.* I went around to all the administrative assistants who helped the managers, introduced myself, and said, "I'm the new intern. Do you have anything you need filed or faxed?" The assistants were delighted that someone was willing to help them get some paper off their desk, so they gave me things to do, and I went to work. I quickly figured out that Handprint didn't even have a filing system, so I created one.

Taking the initiative to help the various assistants out helped me build strong relationships with them. Assistants are the "gatekeepers" in Hollywood (and in many industries). People often only look at the person whose name is on the door while they overlook the assistant, and that's a mistake. I've seen careers crash and burn because someone misjudged who is and isn't important. It's dangerous to disregard or disrespect someone as insignificant because of his or her title. Today's assistant is tomorrow's CEO, and everyone remembers how they were treated on the way to the top—and who treated them well or poorly. Treat the gatekeeper like the person who owns the gate, and you'll go much further.

It was clear that if I was to become successful, I needed to serve everybody without regard for position or title. I did everything I could do to make everyone's day easier. I got their coffee. I got their lunches. I ran errands for them. I copied scripts. I filed papers. I did everything possible to be as helpful as I could be. It worked: Handprint liked me so much that after that school year ended, they wanted to keep me. But the work was still unpaid, so that summer I worked in the dean's office at the USC School of Cinematic Arts and at the Gap at the Beverly Center mall so I could afford to the keep the internship.

I was hungry to become successful in entertainment, and I was willing to do whatever I could (legally and without compromising my faith) to make it happen. I knew that if I was going to be successful, I needed professional and spiritual *grit,* which is defined by the *Journal of Personality and Social Psychology* as "Perseverance and passion for long-term goals." Most people don't fail because they lack ability but because they aren't willing to dig deeply and long enough to see their goals come to fruition. Real success takes guts, courage, and conviction. Even when it's painful, you have to keep pushing because you know where you're going, and you've made up your mind that no force can match your determination.

As the internship progressed, the assistants began to put me in a position to have more responsibility. Then one day, Benny Medina's assistant told him, "DeVon's really good, and he wants to do more for you to get a better sense of how entertainment works."

Benny said, "Cool. Have him drive me."

Hold up. How in the world was driving Benny around a good opportunity? Wasn't it just subservience? No. It was actually the opportunity of a lifetime. Benny was and still is a king in the entertainment business, so while others may have viewed being his driver as demeaning, I knew it was my chance to get what I wanted most: firsthand experience and inside information. Driving Benny around would give me direct access to him and the inner workings of Hollywood—an education more valuable than anything USC could offer.

With that, when I was in the office I would serve as Benny's driver and third assistant. I shuttled a top Hollywood mover and shaker from event to event, meeting to meeting. This was right after The Notorious B.I.G. had been murdered, and Benny was managing Sean "P. Diddy" Combs. Benny would do most of his business in the car on the way to meetings, so I heard how to do business, how to get deals done, how to handle high-level talent, how to handle difficult personalities, and how to market and publicize talent. It was like a mobile master class! I couldn't help but think, *Lord, you do move in incredible ways!*

By serving Benny, I was laying down my foundation. If I wanted to have the kind of influence and impact that Benny Medina had—to wear a crown of my own—I had to help him "carry his crown." So many times, we go into a job saying, "How are my needs going to be met?" But if you want to rise to the top, do the opposite. If your main goal is to be of service to the needs of whomever you work for, your needs will be met in the process.

WHAT IT MEANS TO CARRY A CROWN

Service often has a negative connotation. We want to be the one at the top, calling the shots, making the decisions, getting the glory. But it's useful to step back and look at examples of people who took the service mentality to heart. The greatest example of this is Jesus, who said, ". . . Anyone who wants to be first must be the very last, and the servant of all" (Mark 9:35, NIV). His whole life was an example of someone who could have sought glory and power but instead sought to serve everyone.

Look at King David. In 1 Samuel 16:12, the prophet Samuel anoints David as the next king. But David doesn't immediately go and sit on the throne or look for his crown. After being anointed the next king, David goes and serves the current king, Saul. In Samuel 16:21, it says that Saul makes David his armor bearer, which was a position of service. He had to serve a king before he could be a king!

Take the example of my friend Erica Greve, founder of the charitable organization Unlikely Heroes, which rescues children around the world from sex slavery. She was already in a program at UC Berkeley to become a social worker—a service profession—when she counseled a girl who had been sexually assaulted and decided to serve more intensely by starting an organization to help children in foreign countries who had no one to turn to for help. But even that wasn't enough. Erica chose to serve at an even deeper level by personally going to dangerous places like Nigeria and Burma to counsel and even physically rescue girls who had been kidnapped and sold into slavery. That is a true passion to serve, and it's a passion that has inspired celebrities like Selena Gomez, Babyface, and Macy Gray to become avid supporters of Unlikely Heroes.

In the church, we look at examples like these, and we talk about two important things: destiny and service. We talk about having a destiny that's *ordained by God,* that is, set down by God specifically before we were even a glint in our mother's or father's eyes. That's true. You do have such a destiny. We also learn the importance of service, and how service to others is an important part of following Jesus. Many times, service is defined through the lens of community service, and while serving the community is incredibly important, what is often missed is the lesson about how taking on a service mindset is a requirement to achieve our destiny—and how committing to the process of success itself is essential to achieving a successful career and fulfilling the call on our life. Just because God has ordained that you'll one day be CEO, that doesn't mean you can just expect it to happen without preparation. We saw in the last two chapters how crucial preparation is, and part of that preparation involves service.

Serving someone first is an obstacle that many folks can't get around. Ego can be a career killer. I've come across many people who proclaimed the desire for success but lacked the ability to humble themselves in order to achieve it. Too many people walk into a job thinking, "What can I get, and how can I get it fast?" I've been tempted by similar thoughts more often than I even want to admit. For example, when I became a studio executive, I remember obsessing over how fast I could climb the ladder to become a senior executive, not realizing at the time that no matter how much I wanted it, I was unprepared to do a senior executive's job. We forget that even though being a *superior* might be already written into our life's script, in order to achieve it we must spend some time as a *subordinate.*

As Christians, one of the bedrocks of our faith is service. Jesus commands us to "Love your neighbor as yourself." That means, "Treat your neighbors' needs with the same importance as your own." We serve because we have been called to serve, and to do so in all aspects of our lives: in our relationships, with those who have less than us, and in our careers. When we only apply this idea to community outreach, we miss out on the value this idea can bring to our lives. If we never bring an outreach mentality into our career pursuits, we will be missing out on our God-ordained success. How good is the outreach you provide to your colleagues? How well do you service the needs of your superiors? If you view service as something you do only as part of your church or youth group, you will miss what service can do to help you progress toward the career you've been praying for.

WE ALL SERVE SOMEONE

The other key idea I want you to remember as you think about service is that we all serve someone—usually, *many* "someones." It doesn't matter if you're the CEO of the company. It doesn't matter if you're the owner of a professional sports team. Even as someone might be serving you, you are also serving others—and even as you are serving, other people are serving *you*.

Wait a second. That's a huge idea and bears repeating. *Even as you are serving, you're being served in return.* You might be an assistant to a senior executive at a Fortune 500 corporation and feel like all you do is take care of other people's needs while they get the glory. But the executive you serve is serving you simultaneously. How? By giving you the opportunity to learn, grow, and gain access to the very thing you want to do.

We are, all of us, wound up together in an intricate web of service. Wealthy business owners serve their customers. Legislators serve their constituents (or at least, they're supposed to). Famous actors, musicians, and writers serve their fans. We all serve somebody. So, nobody gets to complain about having to put in their service time because it never ends. You're always going to be serving. It's just that the higher you climb, the better the rewards for that service can become. And the better you become at service, the more successful you will be in the long run.

The danger comes when you forget that in all professions, at all levels, you're in service. You could be at the highest position in your organization or in government, but if you go into it thinking, "I am here to serve myself," not only will you not be as successful as you could be, you may sabotage yourself. Look at the guys at Enron. Look at Bernie Madoff. Look at anyone who's been brought low because they made it all about themselves and stopped caring about the people they were supposed to be serving. That never ever works out in the long run. Here's what I know:

> **When you exalt those whom you serve,**
> **you ultimately exalt yourself.**

False Idols

It's dangerous to believe that service in and of itself makes you virtuous. Serving selflessly and honestly is a virtue, for sure, but serving does not make you a better person than the one you serve. I hear this kind of talk sometimes as a way for people to express their frustration with being in a menial job with low pay: "I'm so much better than so-and-so." True, Matthew 23:11 says, "The greatest among you will be your servant," but that's about all men being equal before God. It doesn't mean that because someone is a success they are automatically egotistical and corrupt—in other words, not worthy of your service. Avoid that kind of thinking and serve as best you can. Great service, ultimately, is the greatest gift you can give others and yourself.

SERVICE VERSUS SERVITUDE

Troy Carter is a friend and former colleague of mine. We both were at Overbrook Entertainment around the same time, assisting Will Smith and James Lassiter in various capacities. The thing about Troy was, he always had a service mentality: he was upbeat, optimistic, and committed to helping whoever needed it the most. Yet even while he serviced others, he had a vision for where he wanted to go and what he wanted to do. After leaving Overbrook he started his own management company because he had a passion for servicing artists. His first major client was Stefani Joanne Angelina Germanotta (a.k.a. Lady Gaga) and the rest was history. Troy's reputation for service led his company, Atom Factory, to become one of the top management firms in entertainment.

Troy also started investing in Silicon Valley, and his passion for service led him to start a tech incubator called Smashd Labs and a venture capital firm called Cross Culture Ventures, both of which help young tech entrepreneurs get started. His service in these two areas has become so successful that Spotify, the $8 billion music streaming service with more than 100 million users, hired him to be their global head of creator services.

I share this with you because I don't want you to think that serving someone else is an anchor around your waist that's preventing you from achieving your destiny. Let's take a few minutes to better understand what service is.

- **Service isn't servitude.** Servitude isn't a word you hear thrown around much anymore, but it's relevant because it is how some people define service without even knowing it. Servitude is defined as "the state of being a slave or completely subject to someone more powerful"—it's involuntary service that humiliates and diminishes the person who serves. It's the slavery that was inflicted on my ancestors and the ancestors of millions of others. However, this is different from hard work and long hours for low pay, which are part of the dues we all must pay to get where we want to be, but are *not* servitude. Service teaches you, and in the best of circumstances, ennobles you. It can even be a calling—something that people who serve others as a career, from doctors and nurses to professional waiters and bartenders, can attest.

There is a big difference between a *service mentality* and a *servitude mentality*. In a service mentality, you can be putting in long hours and working hard, even be unappreciated, but you know that you're getting something out of it—experience, connections, discipline—and you're clear about that. You know that your service does not diminish you but actually builds you up. But in a servitude mentality, you tend to forget who you are and what you were created to do. You allow your circumstances to make you doubt your ability and talent. This mentality is dangerous because you can lose sight of your greater goal and start to believe that you'll never achieve your dreams. This, in turn, can make you resentful, negative, and at times, self-sabotaging. A service mentality will propel you, but a servitude mentality will inhibit you.

- **Service also doesn't mean being servile.** To be *servile* means to be slavishly submissive and lacking in originality. Someone who is servile will debase themselves to get ahead. First of all, nobody respects people who do that—quite the opposite. I found that out in my internship: when God told me to tell the office manager at Handprint about my Sabbath observance, and I finally did, she agreed to work with it. What I've learned in Hollywood—and I believe this is the same in any profession or career—is that people at the top respect those with the confidence of their convictions, even if they disagree with those convictions personally. Why? Because standing on your principles shows you to be a person of character and integrity, the foundational elements of high-level success.

Many people of faith believe that pursuing success in secular environments requires spiritual people to fundamentally compromise what we believe and who we are at our core. But the opposite is true. God doesn't want you to be servile. David wasn't servile; he was a ruler in the making! And you are, too!

- **You can serve someone without having access to them.** If you're not able to get direct access to someone you aspire to be like, it is possible to be of service indirectly. One way is to contribute to the person you want to serve. For example, while I was at Sony Pictures, I was able to work with the great Bishop T. D. Jakes on movies like *Miracles from Heaven* and *Jumping the Broom*. But years before I ever met him, Bishop Jakes's sermons and teachings were a major influence in my life, so much so that I bought many of his books and sermons. If you walk into my office today at home and look at my bookshelves, you'll see almost every one of his books. For years, even from afar, I was doing what I could to be of service to him and assist him in his mission by purchasing his books and encouraging others to do so as well. That's one way to carry a crown.

- **Service requires commitment to the process.** A lot of the time when we're in the lower-echelon service positions that are part of learning any trade, we spend all our time looking forward to when *we're* the ones in power. We say, "Okay, I'm doing this now. But I can't wait until I'm really doing the thing I want to do." Be careful that you don't obsess so much over the future that you neglect your work in the present. Even if you're not where you want to be right now, you're still being prepared, trained, and groomed to fulfill the purpose for your life. Every stage in that process matters.

Sometimes we don't value the time we're serving others because we want things now. We want things when we want them. But I've learned that, when you are in a position of power or influence, the more you end up relying on the lessons you learned during the process you went through to get there. Learn the business by doing it. The better you serve, the better you will be served. The more you will learn, the more people you will impress, and the more opportunities you will have. The process is not just a spiritual thing but a practical thing, too.

• **Traditional ministry isn't the only way to have a service mentality.** Our churches teach that we're here to be of service to God, to be His instruments and carry out one small part of His greater purpose. That's all true. But sometimes, churches take that to mean we can only serve God through traditional ministry. I don't agree with that, and it's one of the ideas that makes people of faith fear going into the secular world and pursuing their God-given ambitions. I look to verses like Colossians 3:23 (NLT), which says, "Work willingly at whatever you do, as though you were working for the Lord rather than for people." We serve God by serving each other. When you go forth and embark upon your career, bust your tail to give your best, and help both the company and the people in it to be *their* best, you are serving God. Don't fear going out into the world and giving your best.

Exodus

Serving others selflessly is the best way to learn and get ahead. However, it's important to not get stuck on one level of service too long. Always be mindful how the current level of service (being an assistant) will lead to the next level of service (being an executive). Remember, the idea is to learn so much and grow so profoundly in mind and spirit through your service that you're ready to graduate to the next level. To avoid staying on one level of service at the expense of your larger destiny, give yourself a target for when you feel it's time to transition. It can be a hard deadline ("By January, I'll have been here for five years, and if I'm not promoted, then it's time to leave") or a soft one ("In 2018, I will lay the groundwork for starting my business"), so long as you set it. A target will keep you focused and remind you that serving need not be a blank check.

A PROPENSITY FOR PATIENCE

Take another look at the story of King David. He was destined to be the next king, yet as we read in 1 and 2 Samuel, he had to endure a process of preparation. God didn't immediately put him on the throne. Before David could be a king, he had to commit to the process that becoming the king would require. His destiny wouldn't come about until he had gone through the process. After Samuel anointed David as the one who would become king, David didn't become the king instantly. In fact, David was sent to serve King Saul, to play the harp, and to be one of the King's armor bearers. Even after David defeated Goliath, he didn't become king; he was forced into exile because King Saul became so jealous of David that he wanted him dead. Some historians believe David was a fugitive for more than fifteen years. In that time, God tested David in order to make him strong and wise, to teach him humility and restraint. Only then did he step into the role of king that he was ordained to fill in his youth.

We live in an impatient world where instant gratification through technology has conditioned us to expect what we want at the moment we want it. This has seeped into our professional lives, so if we don't achieve the success we desire by our deadline, we get frustrated. That frustration can disrupt or even damage the career we are so desperate to have. In my last book, *The Wait,* I talked about the value of delayed gratification and patience in relationships, but it's equally valuable in your career and life pursuits. In life, you don't get extra credit for doing things first.

Unfortunately, we're not good at waiting, especially for opportunity. We've become a country of job hoppers. In April 2016, LinkedIn published a report that stated,

> Over the last 20 years, the number of companies people worked for in the five years after they graduated has nearly doubled. People who graduated between 1986 and 1990 averaged more than 1.6 jobs, and people who graduated between 2006 and 2010 averaged nearly 2.85 jobs.

Meanwhile, *New York* magazine says this on the subject of job hopping:

> In most fields, employers are still wary of people with a track record of jumping around from company to company every year or two, especially once you get past the early part of your career.

Rather than stay in one place long enough to learn how things work, there's a growing tendency to jump ship as soon as the conditions become unfavorable. However, unfavorable circumstances aren't necessarily a signal that it's time to leave your job. Do you know how many unfavorable situations I had to endure on my way to the career I have today? If I had quit when things didn't go my way, I could never have hoped to be where I am now.

"Haste makes waste" is a time-tested adage for a good reason. You get credit in life when you do things well, not fast. I was once location scouting in Beijing and came across an amazing, newly built skyscraper. There was one problem: it was uninhabitable. The contractors had prided themselves on their speed, so they raised the building so quickly that they overlooked important structural concerns. Not long after the building was finished, the foundation began to sink, the building was condemned, and all that money and time were wasted.

Pray against your desire for speed and pray for patience, because patience is a key competitive career advantage. When you put a destination into your GPS, you may hit detours or traffic. But do you worry that you'll never arrive? Of course not. It might take longer than you planned, but you know the destination is locked into your system, and if you stay the course you will get where you want to go. Patience works the same way with your career.

The truth is, you have no idea at this moment what skills, understanding, or personal qualities you'll need at the next stage of your career. If you hurdle over steps because you're obsessed with getting to "next" now, who knows what you'll be missing that might even prevent you from wearing the crown you aspire to wear?

Remember the passage in the Bible where David whines, "When am I going to get on the throne?"? No, you don't, because there isn't one. Impatience wasn't even a thought for David. His attitude was, "I want to be of service. How can I help the kingdom every day?" Pressure, position, high profile—all those things, if you aren't ready for them, will crush you. The process of patient service not only helps those you serve but also puts you in position to walk up the staircase to your success.

Keep stepping, and bring your A game every day. Let "next" take care of itself.

A STAIRCASE, NOT AN ELEVATOR

When I preach, I sometimes say, "Success is not an elevator, it's a staircase." That means there are no shortcuts. We all want to reach the top floor of our destiny, and often we look for an "elevator"— something that can help accelerate the process while bypassing some of the work, the hard steps where we learn and grow. Here's the thing: we want to be at the top, but the altitude feels different up there. If you haven't built up your endurance by climbing, you won't last. If you're complaining about the process and the hard work you have to put in, then you won't be in shape to compete when you reach the top, because *nobody is*. Everyone needs training to endure and succeed.

Taking the stairs gets you in shape to thrive on every floor you stop at on the way to the top. Stop waiting for an elevator and start climbing right now toward your goal. As you get stronger, you'll start being able to take the steps two at a time. After a while, you'll be in shape to start running. Everything you'll learn along the way will build your strength and endurance—your ability to manage where you're going. Let the elevator go. Start taking the stairs. Now.

SPIRITUAL PRINCIPLES, SECULAR SUCCESS

So maybe you're saying to yourself, "DeVon, this is all great. I understand that service is a goal in itself and that it's necessary. Awesome. But how do I use it strategically?" Glad you asked. I'll tell you what I've done in every position I've ever had: looked for the unfilled need or the neglected opportunity, or as I call it:

Look for the seam.

If you're a football fan, you know that a "seam" in football is a vulnerable spot in the downfield defense where the quarterback can slip in a sharp pass and hit a receiver for a big gain. In a garment, the seam is the spot on a piece of clothing where two pieces of fabric are sewn together. It's where you can take the garment apart and change it. In your career, a seam is an underserved or underexploited part of your company or industry. It's an area of tremendous opportunity if you can identify it and come up with a plan to meet whatever needs aren't being met.

I'm always looking for the seam, even now. When I've achieved success, it was because I looked for the seam, asking, "Where can I create change?" When I was a studio executive, I identified a seam at Sony Pictures and devised a plan to exploit it. I saw that there were millions of moviegoers of faith who weren't being offered high-quality major motion pictures that reflected their values. So, I presented a plan to the heads of Sony. I told them that I believed that if we made great films with universal storylines, high production values, and major Hollywood stars, we could unearth a new revenue stream for the company while inspiring millions of people at the box office. They were intrigued by my proposal, and because they knew that I was authentically a person of faith and I had experience making movies they trusted, they had confidence that I could pull it off.

This led to a string of faith-based hits: the romantic comedy *Jumping the Broom* (made for $6 million and grossed $37 million at the box office), *Heaven Is for Real* (made for $15 million and grossed $101 million worldwide), and *Miracles from Heaven* (made for $15 million and grossed $73 million worldwide).

Looking for the seam means being opportunistic even while you're serving. Nothing prevents you from being of service and at the same time being a savvy mover and shaker in your industry. In fact, when you're serving someone higher up the food chain, you're often in the perfect place to see the seams because you have access to tremendous amounts of information. Believe me, I learned more about the entertainment business driving Benny Medina around than I learned in business classes at USC. And the education I received while serving Will and James at Overbrook Entertainment was in many ways more valuable than my undergraduate degree.

Serving someone else can be the greatest opportunity of your life if you take the initiative. Get hungry. Get aggressive. Even today, I'm always saying, "Where's the seam? Where can I be effective? Where can I provoke change or create value? What is no one else doing?" Even while you're serving, look around. Find the unmet need of your company, your job, or an individual, and meet that need with excellence.

Away from the Workplace

If things aren't going well in your life or you just feel discouraged, I have two suggestions. First, pray. Second, get up and go serve someone in need. Helping others is a fantastic mood lifter, so go serve food at a shelter for battered women, lend a hand with a charity that repairs the homes of the elderly and handicapped, read to children in school, mentor a disadvantaged student . . . there are a thousand ways to be of service, and every one of those ways will give you hope, restore your faith in people, and bring you closer to God.

HOW TO LEVERAGE THE POWER OF SERVICE

One of my favorite quotes about service comes from the late Muhammad Ali, who said, "Service to others is the rent you pay for your room here on earth." Service is an obligation, not just something you do as a stepping stone. Learn to take joy in serving well and giving your best. People will notice, and that matters. Because the reality is that no matter where you are in your career, you and a lot of other people are trying to move up the ladder at the same time . . . and it's easy to think of those other people as obstacles in your way. When you focus on your competition, you lose focus on the quality of the service you are providing. If your employer has not experienced the uniqueness of your work and the integrity of your service, you'll become just one more face in the crowd. When an opportunity arises, you'll be passed over because there's nothing distinctive about your work.

But when you go above and beyond the call and *lean into* your service, seeing it rightly as part of God's calling on your life, then you excel. You do things others can't (or won't). You stand out. You get noticed as somebody who cares and works hard—a difference maker. Serving to the best of your ability should become your primary goal because when you help other people get what they want, they will help you get what you want. Here are a few other strategies that can help you turn service into opportunity:

- **Be positive.** People want to work with people they want to be around. So, don't serve begrudgingly. The Bible says, "God loves a cheerful giver" (2 Corinthians 9:7, NIV). So does everybody else. When you have a positive disposition, when you are easy to work with, when people like being around you, they're going to give you more opportunity. It's important to really look at your personality and the vibe you're giving off. I have seen so many people get opportunities not because they were the smartest or most qualified person in the room, but because people liked working with them. *This one piece of advice could help unlock the power of your entire life! Smile!*

- **Take care of the gatekeepers.** I mentioned this before but it's worth repeating. Take care of and pay respect to the people who make the machine run: assistants, receptionists, secretaries, appointment bookers. They're the people who provide that most valuable of commodities: *access.* Gatekeepers control the time and calendars of the most powerful people in every industry, so if you want to get to the guy in the corner office, you have to go through his assistant. These people work hard, and they tend to be terribly unappreciated, so be the person who appreciates them. Be kind, compliment their work, and send thank-you notes, things like that. Treat them with the respect they deserve.

- **Know when it's time to end your term of service.** I've counseled you to focus on service for its own sake, and that's still my advice. However, service is not a blank check. You are carrying that other person's crown for a reason: because it's key to your advancement. But if you're in that position long enough, there will come a time when you've learned everything you can at that level and need to move up or move on. After you've put in the work and earned your keep, it's okay to be clear and honest: *you'd like a new opportunity*. If one isn't forthcoming, or if you're told to wait indefinitely, declare that term of service over. Don't worry about it, but know when that moment has arrived and what you'll do next.

- **If things aren't working out, ask how you can be of better service.** If your career feels stalled and stagnant, don't panic. But also, don't go sending out a thousand resumes or spending a fortune on grad school, not just yet. Instead, ask those you work with and for a simple question: "How can I be of better service?" Remember, it's the quality of your service that creates your value, and when you create value, you get valuable opportunities in return. Be open to honest feedback on the quality of your service and bury your ego when it comes to making the necessary adjustments to do a better job.

When we learn to carry other people's crowns, we are doing what God has called us to do—live lives of service. What's more, we are putting ourselves in valuable positions to learn, study, and grow into the roles we want to be taking on someday.

THOU SHALT

- » Take joy in serving all people well.
- » Ask questions. A position of service is an incredible classroom.
- » Be patient.
- » Look for the seam.

THOU SHALT NOT

- » Feel entitled.
- » Let service in your career interfere with service in your community or vice versa.
- » Forget that by serving man, you put yourself in a position to better serve God.

4

YOU HAVE TO KNOW THE RULES TO PLAY THE GAME

It is a good idea to obey all the rules when you're young just
so you'll have the strength to break them when you're old.

—Mark Twain

I f you don't understand how your business operates, the politics and
the dynamics of recognition, what success means, and who has the
power, you are at a distinct disadvantage. That's one of the rules of
every profession, and that's what this chapter is about. Thinking again
about Daniel, Shadrach, Meshach, and Abednego, we see they had to
learn the rules just like anyone else. Babylon was a system, Hollywood
is a system, and whatever industry you are aspiring to succeed in is a
system as well. The strategy for success the Hebrew boys discovered
was learning the rules of the game and learning how to play the game
with more cunning than everyone else around them, and if you learn
the rules of the game of your system, you will find success too.

We read in 1 Daniel that the four got their internship in Babylon,
where there was a productivity requirement. But as we've discussed, the
position also came with a dietary requirement that went against their

faith. Part of studying the game was saying, "We know we can't eat the same way everyone else eats. Can we meet the professional requirement while still adhering to what we believe?" First, they went to their manager, who said, "Listen, boys. I wish I could help you. But heaven forbid this doesn't work. I'm not only going to lose my job, but I'm going to be killed. So, while I'm sympathetic to your issue, my own desire for self-preservation is greater than my willingness to take a risk on you."

They could have walked away, defeated. But they knew one of the rules of the game, which is *No isn't always no.* They went to their immediate supervisor, which is where they should have gone to begin with. He said, "I will give you ten days to do this. If it doesn't work . . ." In today's terminology, they would be fired, but more permanently. They were given an opportunity to meet the standard, but they bore the responsibility for it.

It was a profound lesson. Daniel, Shadrach, Meshach, and Abednego got what they were looking for, but they also had to check themselves and say, "Wait a minute. Do we really want this? Because now we're going to be held accountable for it." They decided that owning their faith was the way for them to play the game on their own terms, so they agreed. They followed their diet for ten days and at the end of the ten days, they were smarter and more productive than the others in the internship program. So much so that when the internship came to an end, they were so successful that the king accepted them into his service and gave them permanent employment.

KNOW THE RULES

The Hebrew Boys understood that it didn't matter whether they agreed with the rules of Babylon or not. If they wanted the opportunity to apply their spiritual wisdom to achieve secular success, they had to understand the rules and learn to work within them to achieve their goals. Back in Chapter One, we talked about how important it is to study the field you want to be working in. Now let's look at why studying is so important and break down our next Commandment:

You Have to Know the Rules to Play the Game

I'm not diminishing the importance of any career by calling it a game. I understand that some careers—law, medicine, the military, law enforcement—are serious business, even life or death at times. But if you look closely at the path to *advancement* in any career, it looks a lot like a game. There are winners and losers. There's a field of play like the board in a game. There's strategy and traps you can fall into if you're unwary. And there are rules—some written, but many that are unwritten—that you have to follow if you want to have a chance to compete, win, or even stay in the game.

Daniel, Shadrach, Meshach, and Abednego were able to apply their spiritual values to their secular environment because they learned the system. They figured out what the rules were and how those rules fit in with their ethical code, and they pushed those rules as far as they could in order to get the chance to prove that their approach not only was valid but fueled their ascent to success. You can think of the rules as organizing principles that will help you channel your energy in the right places and avoid wasting time. They're also reminders that no matter how you think things *should* work in your profession or your desired line of work, that's not how they actually *do* work. The rules are the ultimate reality check.

I'm going to share some rules that will help you no matter what your talent may be. There are a few quick things you should know about the rules:

- **They don't all carry the same weight.** Depending on your field, some rules will be a lot more important than others. Know which ones they are.

- **They won't all be perfectly suited to your personality.** However, that doesn't mean you can ignore them. It does mean that you may need to grit your teeth when playing that part of the game.

- **They may defy what you think you know.** That's what I've found in the entertainment world. The rules are the codes of the real world that the church is sometimes disconnected from. That doesn't invalidate them; if anything, it makes them even more relevant, because they are critical to helping you move beyond what you think you know and help you understand what really matters.

Okay? Let's talk about the rules of the game.

RULE #1: EVERYONE IS CONCERNED ABOUT SELF-PRESERVATION

The immediate supervisor of Daniel, Shadrach, Meshach, and Abednego was willing to go out on a limb to allow them to apply their dietary beliefs, but their main manager was not. He was more concerned with protecting his own neck than with allowing his subordinates to do something that may or may not have increased their productivity. His desire for self-preservation came before everything else. This is important to understand when you are navigating your career.

People whom I've counseled about their life and careers have often missed this key rule and how to apply it to make the right moves or navigate the system they're in. You need to learn how to think from a bird's-eye point of view and say, "These are the issues, and these are people's concerns. How can I alleviate somebody's concern and still get what I'm looking for, which is opportunity?" If you go after opportunity without understanding that the people you work for have things they want, you will have a hard time getting that opportunity. Even if you do get it, you will have a political target on your back.

Going back to the Hebrew boys, Daniel understood this rule well. When he approached his immediate superior to negotiate the opportunity to eat differently, he provided a time frame: "Try us out for ten days on a simple diet of vegetables and water. Then compare us with the young men who eat from the royal menu. Make your decision on the basis of what you see" (Daniel 1:12–13, MSG). Providing a time frame was essential to getting the "yes" because Daniel understood the needs of his supervisor and framed his request in a way that would fit with those needs.

To become successful in life, you have to be strategic and smart. Jesus was smart. He was strategic. He was thoughtful. He spent thirty years studying the environment, the politics, the economy, the culture, of where he would work and ultimately minister. He learned everything about the game he would play, including what the other players wanted. Before he made a play for power, he made himself into a strategic warrior.

This concern for self-preservation doesn't have to come from a place of malice or self-centeredness. According to the *Employee Well Being Study* from *HRO Today* magazine and Yoh Recruitment Process Outsourcing, we live in a time when the potential for job promotion and raises and employee trust are at historic lows. This translates into most people (especially those in positions of power) being hypersensitive about their job security. Just like you, they have families to provide for, mortgages to pay, and car payments to make. When they are evaluating their staff and deciding whom to stand behind, this plays a huge role.

Church doesn't always prepare us for that reality. It's not going to be enough just to walk onto a movie set or into advertising, law, or venture capital and say, "God's going to work it out for me, praise the Lord." As we've learned, God is actively working for us, but we must do our part and study the people we work for and with. Being aware of and sensitive to the underlying current of self-preservation can even give you an advantage over people who have more experience than you do.

Don't deceive yourself. There will always be some selfless people who will help you because they care. But by and large, you will be rewarded based on how you help others reach their goals. There's another difficult truth to absorb, which is that early in your career, you might do terrific work that furthers a superior's self-interest but receive no reward or recognition for it. That's common, unfair, and unlikely to change. How do you avoid becoming bitter and cynical?

First, don't always expect recognition. Don't assume that if you make a superior or mentor look good, it will always translate to direct recognition from them; sometimes it does, sometimes it doesn't. However, early in my career, I learned that even if I didn't get the reward or recognition I was looking for from my direct superior, I still was set up to succeed because this understanding was extremely useful in my subsequent jobs. Second, keep your head down and continue doing great work. Remember, praise, recognition, and fame from others isn't your main goal; you are working as though you were working for the Lord. Eventually, you will be recognized beyond even your deepest ambitions.

RULE #2: NO ISN'T ALWAYS NO

It depends whom you get the "No" from. The Hebrew Boys got a "No" from their manager, but they went to their immediate supervisor, who said, "I'm going to give you ten days. And if it doesn't work, you're done." Which meant they would be dead. That's a "be careful what you wish for" scenario, isn't it?

Have you ever heard the saying, "No one ever got fired for saying no"? Every creative industry uses it because any creative idea—whether it's for a movie, a book, or a piece of software—is inherently risky and hard to visualize. If you approach someone with an idea or an offer, and they can't visualize it being successful, they're going to say "No." That does not necessarily mean your purpose is incorrect, your idea is a bad one, or your offer isn't worthy of consideration. It might mean that particular person doesn't connect with your vision or doesn't have the vision to see the value in you or your proposal. That doesn't translate into a definitive "No" that derails your destiny.

Consider these superstars who heard "No" in their careers:

- **Walt Disney** was fired from the *Kansas City Star* in 1919 because, his editor said, he "lacked imagination and had no good ideas."

- **Elvis Presley** is one of the bestselling musical artists of all time. But back in 1954, Elvis was still a nobody, and Jim Denny, manager of the Grand Ole Opry, fired him after just one performance, telling him, "You ain't goin' nowhere, son. You ought to go back to drivin' a truck."

- **Kerry Washington,** before making it on *Scandal,* had done two pilots. Both shows got picked up, but a different actress replaced Kerry in both shows.

- **Harrison Ford,** one of the leading box office superstars of all time, was told by the executives on his first film that he simply didn't have what it takes to be a star.

- **Sidney Poitier,** after his first audition, was told by the casting director, "Why don't you stop wasting people's time and go out and become a dishwasher or something?" Poitier vowed to show him that he could make it, going on to win an Oscar and becoming one of the most respected actors in the business.

- **Stephen King** saw his first book, the iconic thriller *Carrie,* receive thirty rejections, finally causing him to give up and throw it in the trash. His wife, Tabitha, fished it out and encouraged him to resubmit it, and the rest is history. King is now one of the best-selling authors of all time.

- **Steve Jobs** was fired from his own company. On returning, all he did was create the iPod and iPhone and lay the foundation for the world's most valuable company.

Some of the most influential people in every business were catapulted to success because someone told them "No." It's happened to me, too. Do you think every script I've liked and pitched has become a film or TV series? No. Do you know how many times I've wanted to speak somewhere and I was told "No"? I was told

"No" by the USC School of Cinematic Arts. Even now, I hear "No" frequently, and sometimes, that's a good thing. Sometimes, either your ideas (or mine) are not fully developed, the timing isn't right, or perhaps we're not asking for "Yes" from the right person. That's okay. You discard what doesn't work, learn why it didn't work, retain that lesson, and keep going. But more important, being told "No" is the path to "Yes." There is no one who hasn't had doors slammed in their face—not in film, literature, art, business, sports, politics, you name it. Being denied or turned down should motivate you to keep developing and improving your script, business plan, resume, presentation, or whatever you're using to put your best foot forward.

My basic rule here is this:

**Don't let the fear of a "No" frighten you
away from going after "Yes."**

Too often, we're so afraid of hearing "No" that we don't pursue what God has put in our heart. If God has called you to do it, then every "No" gets you that much closer to God's "Yes." Also, if you believe in what God has called you to do, don't take "No" as the final answer. Revise and regroup, but keep pushing. Ask someone else. Ask one hundred someone elses until you get "Yes."

Here's one qualifier, though: be clear about whether what you're pursuing is His will or your will. If you keep hearing "No" again and again, start asking why. If after careful consideration and prayer, it's revealed that what you are pursuing isn't God's will for you after all, accept it and move on. There's nothing wrong with moving on to the next thing that He has planned for you.

RULE #3: YOU WILL FIND ALLIES

Hollywood has a reputation for being cutthroat and hyper-competitive, and to some extent that's true. Jobs are few while the number of people who dream about working in entertainment is off the charts, so naturally, there's a lot of competition. The same is true of any field where the rewards are substantial and the work is perceived as desirable. In this kind of environment, it can seem hard to find people who will have your back. But if you're a person of strong values and character, you will find them.

Your values are like magnets that attract people who will be compelled to help you because of your convictions. I found allies from the very beginning. They were USC professors who believed in me, mentors who guided me, and early bosses who gave me a chance. One of the discoveries that sustained me during the early days of trying to build a career in Hollywood was finding that, despite what many people in my church had told me about Hollywood being a place of sin and moral compromise, there were terrific people everywhere I looked. Not all of them were or are Christians. Don't let your faith blind you to the reality that there are plenty of virtuous, moral people who have never set foot in a church (as well as some folks who might kneel every weekend in church but whom I would think twice about trusting).

Every business is a pyramid; there are a lot more people at the bottom looking for handholds to start climbing than there are at the top occupying the corner offices and taking home seven-figure bonuses. So, if you're starting your career climb, you have plenty of company. Talk to people. Band together for support and ideas. Getting up that pyramid is rough; lean on each other. Have each other's back. Be happy for each other's success.

Of course, you don't want everyone as an ally. There's a great line from the film *The Adventures of Priscilla, Queen of the Desert* (where most of us first got to know the brilliant Hugo Weaving and Guy Pearce) that sums this up perfectly: "There are two things I don't like about you—your face." In any field, you will find people who cannot be trusted and a few who might actively try to undermine you. They are rare, but they're out there. Reach out and build alliances, but have your eyes open. If you come across someone who appears unable to maintain alliances or who has a reputation for being untrustworthy, that's probably a person you should avoid.

False Idols

One thing about the rules is that, while you can choose to follow them or not follow them, you do yourself a disservice if you act like they don't exist. The rules are the collective product of people who have worked in your field for decades, perhaps even centuries. They are codes of conduct that are permanent parts of the landscape, so if you don't like one of them, that's okay. But before you disregard a certain rule, understand it. When you master the game, you might be able to apply a rule in a new way. But be careful about deciding that the rules don't apply to you, because they apply to everyone. No exceptions.

RULE #4: YOU WILL BE HELD ACCOUNTABLE

Just as the Hebrew Boys were held accountable for their decision to pursue their faith-prescribed dietary approach, you will be held accountable for your choices and performance. Incidentally, that's not always negative; accountability simply means that you will reap the fruits of what you sow. If you put in long hours and do terrific work, accountability might mean being rewarded with advancement. However, good or bad, accountability always means this:

**Everything you do creates expectations
about what you'll do next.**

From the minute you step into an office, studio, school, or hospital to start a job, you begin creating expectations, and you will be held accountable according to how you uphold those expectations. If you go above and beyond to solve a problem for your boss during the first week, she's probably going to expect that kind of performance from you all the time. If you slack off and drop the ball on a project, people might expect you to be unreliable until you prove otherwise. So, accountability isn't just being called on the carpet for what you do right or wrong but also having to be mindful about the expectations your work creates in others.

Some smart questions to ask as you move through your career:

- What expectations are my work, choices, and professionalism creating, especially for the people who can make decisions that harm or help my career?

- Am I living up to the positive expectations and how can I do that better?

- How can I shed any negative expectations?

The other tricky thing about accountability is that it occurs whether you are aware of it or not. Everything you do has an impact on how you are perceived and the opportunities you're afforded, even if there's no call to the boss's office or big promotion. Accountability can be loud or it can be quiet, but it's always there.

RULE #5: CHARACTER IS PERSUASIVE

Selflessness, reliability, morals—it's easy to be cynical about them and call them old-fashioned, but don't be fooled. People at every level, in every business, all the way to the penthouse or corner office, care deeply about and respect people who are honest, keep their word, and live according to a set of strong moral and ethical precepts. People are people everywhere, and we all want to work with colleagues we can trust, who care about us, and who do the right thing.

Because you come into the world of your career from a background in the church, that makes your faith-based moral center a powerful advantage. Even if you have no experience, even if you're starting at the bottom rung of the ladder, you can always be generous, just, kind, dependable, hardworking, of service, and a good listener. None of those qualities requires an advanced degree or any sort of apprentice program; just be who you are. Over time, you will find that people recognize, then appreciate, and finally reward those qualities.

What can make this difficult is when you see people passing you on the career climb who do not display good character. They gossip, for instance, or undercut their peers. It happens. But in the long run, those people always fail. *Always.* And even if they didn't, you're in this for more than career advancement; you're in this to become the person God wants you to be. Even if your ascent is a little bit slower because you play by the rules, it will be more sure and sustainable, and you'll appreciate who you are becoming as you climb the ladder to the top.

Exodus

The rules impact everyone. What if you find yourself working for an individual (or company) who believes the rules don't apply to them? Who thinks it's okay to lie, cheat, intimidate, and harass as a path to success? No matter how big the carrot is, no matter how powerful the person in charge claims to be, leave. The people you associate with affect you, and if you stay with a person, organization, or company that inherently does business in the wrong way, it can impact you negatively for years to come.

RULE #6: THERE ARE ALWAYS LEVERS OF POWER

Levers of power are pressure points that, if pushed, can make things happen. They exist in every profession. In Hollywood, a great idea is an important pressure point, because every movie and TV show begins with an idea—sometimes expressed as a screenplay, sometimes expressed just as a short, written summary called a *treatment*. Even if you're new to Hollywood, with no connections and nothing on your resume, a great idea can make things happen for you. Agents are also levers of power because they can open doors and establish relationships with important decision-makers.

Every field has its levers of power. In Washington, they are lobbyists for special interests. In Silicon Valley, they're the tech journalists who can turn an unknown startup into a venture-capital darling overnight. In academia, a key lever of power is getting your work published in the right peer-reviewed journal. They exist in your field, too. The key questions are, what are they and how can you push them to your benefit?

Finding these levers is a matter of looking in the right place. What are the events that seem to make things happen in your world? What makes the money flow? What attracts influential people to a company or event? What gets attention and commands respect? Once you can answer those questions, the next obvious question is, how can you push those levers to your own benefit? For example, let's say you work in the New York fashion world, and you notice that the journalists who cover Fashion Week not only get access but get their work read around the world and sometimes get career opportunities. That's a lever. So, you start your own blog about Fashion Week, leverage what contacts you have, and write some of your own original coverage of the shows and new lines. If you do great work, maybe you get noticed, get some business cards from heavy hitters, and even get some job interviews.

Figure out what the levers are and how to use them. Then you work on getting close enough to push.

RULE #7: THE PLAYERS AREN'T ALWAYS WHO THEY APPEAR TO BE

People are levers of power. The tricky part is that the people who can really make things happen for you aren't always the people you think. For example, in Hollywood, the obvious power players are the studio executives, the directors, the big-name actors, and the powerful agents. And it's true that those people have a great deal of power. However, they aren't always the ones to set the wheels in motion for a new film or to give an aspiring actor or writer an opportunity. Often, the people who move heaven and earth to actually make things happen on the ground are the administrative assistants, the personal assistants, and the crew.

The reality is that sometimes the people with the most important titles are the ones least able to provide opportunities. I know that seems ironic but it's true. For instance, the CEO of a corporation might be so distanced from the day-to-day work of the company that he or she doesn't really know which employees are doing great work. However, a manager further down the chain of command might know who the budding superstars in the company are—and which opportunities best suit them. If you work in a school, your principal might be too busy to understand what you're capable of, but the assistant principal might become your champion.

My definition of power players has nothing to do with title or salary. Real power players are people who can pick up the phone or send an email and get the wheels turning, and those aren't always the people in the big offices but the people below them who do the scheduling, make all the phone calls, and have the experience and relationships in the industry to make things happen the way they're supposed to.

My advice? Be a person of morals, ethics, discipline, and high performance to everyone from the people in the C-suite down to the people on the front lines and in the cubicles.

Away from the Workplace

Every arena of human activity has rules, including marriage and friendships. You need to learn these rules and adhere to them because they're vital for being happy in these areas. For example, one of the rules of friendship I follow is that friends don't bad-mouth each other behind each other's backs. We're supportive and, if the situation calls for it, critical. But we don't run each other down. If you can't obey that rule, then you need to find some new friends. What are the rules in the other areas of your life—relationships, family, school, church? Are you honoring them?

RULE #8: PATIENCE PAYS

This rule is slightly tricky to manage. It might even appear that I'm contradicting myself. In the past, I've said that you should go after your career goals with ambition and vigor. Now I'm counseling you to be patient. Why the change?

There is no change. You should always be aggressive about pursuing what you want, but there are times when the career path you desire is simply not within your reach—not yet, anyway. Those are times for patience. Do you all the right things, build the right relationships, and then be patient—because that's all you can do. Sometimes building a career means planting the seeds and waiting for harvest time to come. Meanwhile, you sharpen the tools and prepare yourself, but it's out of your hands and in God's hands.

Don't be passive. Passivity means you don't speak up, fail to demand credit where it's due, or tolerate behavior that goes against your values. Be actively assertive about who you are and how you want to be in your career of choice. Demonstrate your character, put yourself in a position to have your work seen, and then put your head down and just get things done. It takes time for certain things to manifest. Remember, it took me eighteen years to finally achieve my dream of becoming a producer.

RULE #9: PEOPLE ARE FICKLE ... DON'T TAKE IT PERSONALLY

People can change on a dime depending on how much they think they need you at any given moment. Don't base your self-worth on attention or approval from anyone you know. I've seen people make that mistake many times, and it's devastating to watch. One day, some friends of mine were "in" with a group with whom they found validation. Then, for no apparent reason, that group no longer found the same value in the relationship with my friends. Just like that, phone calls stopped being returned, projects stopped flowing, and the relationship went cold. My friends were crushed. It was difficult to see people I cared about deal with the pain, humiliation, and confusion of no longer being in a relationship with people they thought valued them, only to find out that they were disposable.

Your self-worth should be based on one factor: being the person God created you to be. In other words:

You are who you are no matter what people say or do.

The reality of life is that when you're in the spotlight, adoration can turn to anger in the blink of an eye. In March 2017, *Billboard* published an article about Chris Brown that said, "Many people who are thrust into the spotlight [as kids] are traumatized when they make a mistake and realize how fast that love turns to hatred. When I look in Chris' eyes, I think that's some of the pain." None of us is immune to this, and the more public you are, the worse it is. It is devastating when people turn on you.

There is nothing wrong with having a strong network of associates—in fact, it's a critical part of a thriving career. However, your self-esteem should not rest on those associations, because they are usually matters of convenience. True friends will stick with you through thick and thin, but you will also encounter many who want to be around you because you are enjoying a degree of success—and when that success fades, so will their interest in you.

Years ago, I met with singing superstar Ciara, and she told me, "People shake your hand differently when you have a hit song on the radio. They treat you differently when you don't." My wife, Meagan, said, "There are times when I have a hit movie and I go to an event and I'm escorted to the front of the line. There are times when I don't have a hit film and I'm told to wait in the back of the line." The point is, people are fickle and fame is fleeting. Don't be a different person based on who's in your corner or who's returning your calls. Be the same version of yourself no matter whom you're with.

Part of the reason for this is self-protection. If you don't base your self-esteem on other people's approval, you won't be as devastated when someone you thought was a friend turns out to be something else. Letting such betrayals make you question your worth and who you are can lead to bitterness, anger, and resentment, and those emotions can lead to long-term professional, emotional, and spiritual damage. There's an old saying: "Friends are for a reason or a season." Friends who are with you for a season will come and go as your and their fortunes rise and fall, but friends who are there for a reason will be friends no matter what happens. Learn the difference between the two and remember that God's approval is ultimately all you need.

RULE #10: FRUSTRATION IS DISRUPTIVE

Frustration—a feeling of dissatisfaction, often accompanied by anxiety or depression, resulting from unfulfilled needs—will derail every dream and goal you have because it will make you believe that what you're waiting for will never happen. How often do we find ourselves frustrated because things aren't progressing as we'd hoped for in our life and career? If you're anything like me, then the answer is *often*. Over my twenty years in entertainment, there have been times that I've been frustrated to the point of tears. Early on, my desire to succeed was consuming, but I felt like success was nowhere in sight.

Frustration is disruptive because it's like a virus in your spirit. One of the most important areas it impacts negatively is your disposition and your energy. When you are working with others, do you put out positive energy or negative energy? Maintaining a positive disposition even in times of hardship works like a magnet, attracting more people and opportunities to you; a negative disposition does the opposite. When you're frustrated, people can tell. Being frustrated wastes energy and time. Instead of presenting your best self and doing your best work, your frustration compromises you. In your impatience to make success happen, you take shortcuts, don't deliver your best work, and alienate people who in other circumstances might be allies.

Even now, there are many things I'm hoping to achieve and believe will manifest. Yet when I don't see them happening fast enough, I'm guilty of becoming frustrated. Frustration zaps my energy and my time. I've spent weeks lost in frustration and crippled by it. I couldn't move forward or even think forward because I was so upset with what wasn't happening in my life. Resist the temptation to give in to frustration, because at its core, frustration is an expression that you don't believe that God's plan for you will really manifest. But it will. God has a plan and a time when things are destined to come to pass in your life and your career. If you find yourself getting frustrated, stop and look at what's in front of you and ask yourself: "What's the best I can do right now with what I have?"

Here's a prayer that might also help you get through:

THE FRUSTRATION PRAYER

Dear Almighty God,
   Please help me deal with this virus called Frustration. I'm frustrated because I'm not where I want to be, I'm frustrated

because I know I'm talented and have a calling on my life, but I don't see how anything You've promised me will ever come to pass. I'm frustrated because I'm tired of being overlooked and passed on. I'm frustrated because I'm tired of being told I'm not good enough. I'm frustrated because I have a burning desire to be successful yet it doesn't seem like it's going to happen. I'm frustrated because I never can seem to catch a break. I'm frustrated because I keep seeing a vision of the life I want to live but the life I currently live looks nothing like it yet.

Please, my God, help me. I'm crying out to You from the depths of my soul! I need peace to sustain me during the times when my frustration is so intense I start to lose my faith. I come against the frustration that seeks to derail my very existence! No weapon formed against me will prosper! I claim every good and perfect gift You've already planned for my life and I submit my career to You! You said Your word would not return to You void and anything I ask for in the name of Jesus, You would do, so in the name of Jesus, I claim victory over this frustration that threatens to disrupt my God-ordained destiny!

I claim this peace in the mighty name of Jesus.
AMEN!!!

HOW WILL YOU KNOW YOU'RE WINNING?

Now that we've reviewed the rules, the next logical question is how do we know when we're winning? If you play a game, you do it to win, and I assume that's true in your career, too. But what does winning look like for you, and how will you know when you've won?

When you've reached your goal, how will you know? What will change? How will you change? Each one of us has to define what winning is for us. The danger is that when you look at someone else's life or career and see their version of winning, without doing an assessment for yourself, you can go down the wrong path. With Daniel, Shadrach, Meshach, and Abednego, winning meant continuing their study in Babylon, yet doing it in a way that didn't compromise their faith. Winning wasn't, "We want to get the job and outshine the person we're working next to. We want to become managers within the provenance of Babylon."

When you look at David, what was winning? Winning was, "Restoring honor to my nation by defeating the villain that is threatening that honor." Once he won, his ultimate win was unifying the kingdom of Israel and bringing Israel and Judah together.

You must define winning on your terms. It could be, "I don't want to be the president of the division. I love my job, and I don't want the stress. This job allows me the quality of life I want." Winning is about more than money and position; it's about the quality of your life and operating in the seat of your purpose. My definition of success is *peace,* so for me, winning is having what creates the most peace in my life and in my spirit.

To finish the game analogy: *know what you're playing for.* If you don't know what you're playing for, then you will spend years aimlessly working at a job with no idea about what matters and doesn't matter. When I first got in the industry, I knew I wanted to produce and be autonomous. I was playing for that from day one. Even while I was in the studio system, I never lost sight of what winning meant to me. I would say to myself, "The more opportunity I can get, the more experience I can get. The more experience I can get, then the more authority I can get. Eventually, the more authority I can get, the better chance I will have to become a producer. And when I become a producer, I can make the films that inspire hope and change."

Winning starts with opportunity. Opportunity leads to experience, and then to authority. Opportunity-Experience-Authority: with these three factors in hand, you can play the game and be certain of winning.

THOU SHALT

» Know the game you're playing, then learn the rules.
» Respect other people's games and goals.
» Learn the power players.

THOU SHALT NOT

» Be passive.
» Compromise on what makes you a good person.
» Lose sight of why you're playing.

5

YOUR GUT IS HIDING GOD

Warren Buffett told me once, "Always follow your gut. When you have that gut feeling, you have to go with it; don't go back on it."
—LeBron James

God will sometimes give you a feeling that you have to follow: a gut instinct. The movie business was founded primarily on gut-instinct decision-making. One of the things that has changed over time: entertainment has become more corporate. Legendary Hollywood journalist Peter Bart recently wrote an article for Deadline.com entitled "Conglomeration Is Snuffing Out Courage in Hollywood." In it, he quotes an industry insider who says, "Hollywood was far better off before the corporate giants annexed the studios and networks." It's a compelling argument. The overall quality of movies has suffered because fewer people are making decisions based on instinct and intuition while more seem to be making decisions based on quarterly earnings, analytics, and market forecasts. However, as much as Hollywood is a business, it's also fundamentally a creative and artistic enterprise.

Great work arises from gut instinct as much as—or more than—it does from data and consensus. When you don't trust your instincts and follow them, you might do something that makes sense intellectually, but it won't have the impact you intended because it's not actually the choice that's in your spirit.

One person in the business who's thrived on his gut instinct is my good friend and occasional producing partner Joe Roth. He is one of the most successful people in Hollywood, and we were fortunate to work together on *Heaven Is for Real* and *Miracles from Heaven*. He used to be chairman of Twentieth Century Fox and the Walt Disney Company. In 2000, he started his own studio, Revolution Studios, which made hits like *Hellboy* and *xXx* with Vin Diesel.

One of the keys to Joe's long-term success is his ability to trust his gut. Years ago, he had a strong urge to get into the world of professional soccer and had a vision to establish Seattle as the soccer capital of the U.S. He paid $30 million for a team license from Major League Soccer (MLS) and started Seattle Sounders FC. More than eight years later, according to the *Oregonian,* Seattle has indeed become the soccer capital of the U.S., and Seattle Sounders FC is worth $285 million, making it the most valuable team in the MLS—all because Joe had a gut feeling and acted on it.

Joe had a gut feeling about *Heaven Is for Real.* He found the book and brought it to me when I was an executive for Sony. We made it into a movie for $15 million and it grossed more than $100 million worldwide. Joe has consistently lived by his gut instinct in the face of conventional information that told him otherwise—in the face of doubters who've said, "Oh, that's not smart, I wouldn't do that." Over time, his gut has paid off tremendously. Yes, it's important to look at information, yet you have to be willing to factor that into what your gut is telling you. That brings me to this Commandment:

Your Gut Is Hiding God

We're told to listen for the voice of God speaking to us, guiding us toward our purpose. But despite what you may have been told, God doesn't usually shout. He doesn't speak as a voice from a burning bush like He did to Moses. Most of the time, His voice is subtle and organic, a voice that we recognize—the voice speaking from your gut instinct, compelling you to do something that, at first glance, might not even make sense.

But if you understand that God speaks in your gut, it makes perfect sense. Let's look at what that voice sounds like.

TRUSTING MY GUT IN MY SONY EXODUS

Too often, we don't trust our gut. We look to other people to tell us what to do, to validate our instincts with facts so that we feel more comfortable. But usually, that doesn't work out. I believe gut instinct is God speaking to us in a way that challenges our intellect—that reminds us that for all we know and can figure out, we're not smarter than the Creator. When you pray and ask God for guidance, sometimes He won't answer because He's already given you your answer in the form of your instinct.

Now, here's the tricky part. Most of us are willing to follow God's voice speaking in our gut—as long as it tells us to do something that we're already comfortable doing. It's the ultimate confirmation bias. But when our gut tells us to do something unexpected, risky, or that flies in the face of what society or the church thinks we should do, we're unwilling to trust it. That's where prayer can be a doublecheck of your instinct. You say, "Okay, Lord, I really feel this is what I'm supposed to do. I'm going to pray on it and look for confirmation." But that confirmation does not always come in a conventional form.

This was brought home to me in a big way when I moved my company, Franklin Entertainment, from Sony Pictures Entertainment to Twentieth Century Fox. The way this works in Hollywood is if you're a producer, and you sign a "first look" producing deal with a studio, you're an independent contractor, but the studio pays for your overhead (which includes things like employee salaries and office space). In return, you give that studio first crack at any movies you're developing. It's a nice deal, but by the beginning of 2016, my gut was telling me that it might be time to move on.

A bit of backstory: I found the book proposal for *Miracles from Heaven* at the end of the summer in 2014. I developed the script with amazing screenwriter Randy Brown, and while we were working on the script, all the computers within Sony Pictures were hacked as an act of protest against the movie *The Interview,* which poked fun at North Korean dictator Kim Jong Un. The hack was devastating because countless private emails from Sony's top executives were leaked. It was so severe that Amy Pascal, chairperson of the Motion Picture Group of Sony Pictures Entertainment, lost her job at the beginning of 2015. Amy hired me as an executive back in 2005 and was a tremendous source of support and guidance for my career and so many others on the Sony lot. The former chairman of Twentieth Century Fox and the then-president of TriStar Pictures, Tom Rothman, was selected to come in and succeed Amy.

I turned in the draft screenplay for *Miracles from Heaven* at the beginning of 2015, and even with the regime change, everyone at Sony felt that it was a great script and would be a good film. We got award-winning director Patricia Riggen to direct and Jennifer Garner came on board to star along with Queen Latifah. We finished the film at the end of the summer of 2015, tested it in front of an audience that fall, and it tested great. Everyone felt like we had a film that could be big at the box office.

Then, in January of 2016, right as we were finishing *Miracles from Heaven*, I had a feeling that it might be time to find a new home. Even though I had been with Sony for over ten years, it was like God was yelling in my spirit that the Sony chapter was over. At first, I couldn't believe what I was hearing but I decided to listen anyway. I listened to God as He was speaking in my gut. It became a lightbulb moment. It was scary but it was time for me to go. This was another moment where God was saying, "Get out of the boat!"

WAKE-UP CALL

That was a valuable wake-up call. Sometimes we look for favorable conditions as evidence that God is involved in events, but that's not always the case. Sometimes God shows up in unfavorable things, the things we don't want to go through. Turbulence on the job. Downsizing. Relationships ending. God will use those because when we're comfortable, we get complacent and talk ourselves into believing that things will work out. When we're uncomfortable, we're more likely to act.

That spiritual punch to the gut is like smelling salts. Why does someone give you smelling salts? Because you're unconscious. Once you're awakened, you can see things as they are, and seeing things as they are—not as you wish they could be—is the only way that you'll take the risk of leaving what you have for something better. As long as you have delusions that your current situation will improve someday, you're exposed and vulnerable.

I went to my representatives and said, "I think it's time for me to leave Sony." They put the word out and a number of studios were interested, including Fox. While that was happening, *Miracles from Heaven* came out and did great at the box office.

With that wind at my back, I was able to get out of my Sony deal and I could feel my gut saying, "Fox is the place," but my head wasn't sure. What do you do when your gut and your head are saying completely different things?

False Idols

Listening to your gut is essential, but it's possible to take it too far: acting only on impulse and not employing critical thinking or reason at all. People who do that tend to leap before they look in every situation, which can be detrimental if you're running a department or a company. Have you ever had a crazy idea about work that you didn't act on but that would've turned out to be a disaster if you had? My tool for avoiding this is simple: if I have a harebrained idea in my gut, I stop. I pray. I see if the same instinct is still speaking to me—and still seems worth trying— the next day. Gut impulses that don't come from God usually lose their allure fast. Instincts that are from God continue speaking to us and often grow louder. Those are the ones to listen to.

LEARNING TO LIVE WITHOUT A NET

I prayed, "Lord, I know You didn't bring me this far to leave me. I trust that if I follow what I believe You are saying in my gut, then I will make the right decision. I'm looking for You to give me confirmation once I do." God replied, *I've got this.* A couple of days later, Fox made an offer and I took it. I've been working with Fox since November of

2016, and it has been even greater than I hoped it would be. I'm doing movies with all divisions, producing television series, and more.

The affair was a reminder that at the end of the day, if we're faithful, we have to follow what God tells us to do and trust that we will be okay, even if at the time, we don't understand how we will be okay. God knows what lies ahead for us, and if we let Him drive, He won't steer us wrong. You know those irresistible gut instincts that you can't seem to shut out, the ones that badger you day and night about a person or job or creative idea? That's God whispering, bypassing the rational part of your brain that insists it knows what's going on, and talking to your spirit, saying, "Trust me. Do this. Don't be afraid of the risk."

Some other important things to know about acting on your gut instinct:

- **When God says move, move.** God doesn't hold windows open for you forever. There's a timeliness to moving on whatever He has put in your gut; if you hesitate for too long, what He has in mind can disappear. My window was small and I acted while it was open, which made all the difference in the world. What are the windows God has opened for you that you've been too afraid to go through?

- **Anticipate discomfort.** Earlier, I made the point that God doesn't give us things that we have the power to get for ourselves. This is a corollary to that: *God rarely asks us to act in ways that we find comfortable.* When He speaks in your gut, He's going to push you in directions that take you out of your comfort zone: leaving your job, breaking up with someone you're dating, moving to a new city, standing up to someone who treats you unfairly, being of service to others in a way that's difficult or inconvenient, taking a project in a bold, new creative direction. Assume right now that when your gut instinct speaks to you in a way that you can't ignore, you're going to feel uncomfortable. Get used to the idea, and know that it's a sign that God is behind the feeling.

- **Take irreversible action.** We're all human. We all feel fear. We all doubt. God knows that, which is why He rewards people who trust His voice in their gut and step out in faith. But even if your faith is strong, you might be tempted to backslide, to retreat, to say, "Never mind" to a life-changing opportunity when things get tense. Know a great way to prevent that? Take an action that leaves you no path back to where you were. Resign from your job. Put your house on the market. Clean out all the unhealthy food in your house before you start your new diet and training for that marathon. Don't give yourself a way to backtrack. When the only way you can go is forward, you will be amazed at how bravely and steadily you will progress.

  I see this mentality come into play with people who want to step out into the freelance world as writers, designers, photographers, you name it. That's scary, but it can be incredibly rewarding. But you might never do it if you have the safe harbor of a job you can retreat to. Sometimes, you don't know what you can do until you give yourself no choice but to do it.

- **If you build it, He will come.** The thing you have to remember about gut instincts—this is one of the things that makes them so challenging—is that they won't make sense to anyone else. So, you'll meet resistance, especially if you're doing something that requires creativity: making a movie, writing a book, starting a business, and so on. You'll be like Ray Kinsella, the Kevin Costner character in *Field of Dreams*, plowing under your corn to build a baseball field while everyone around you tells you you're insane and your bank threatens to foreclose. This is where you need to have faith and ignore the naysayers, especially the ones who try to refute your idea with facts and figures. Understand, *ideas from the gut always look crazy to people who never make decisions from their gut.*

- **Don't turn off your brain.** Trust your gut to guide the big moves, but use your logic and reason to attend to the details. My instinct, brought to me from God, sparked my decision to make my exodus from Sony. But after I made that life-changing call, I relied on reason as well as instinct to get me home. I weighed the pros and cons and carefully considered what I wanted from my new deal. Jumping into any deal with any studio, regardless of the terms, while shouting, "God told me to do it!" would've been foolish. God gave you critical thinking skills and intelligence to be used; don't turn them off just because your instinct has a loud voice.

  Go back to my advice to pray, but prepare, and use your reason and intelligence to give you an edge. Want to develop your engineering skills so you can advance in your company? Get involved in "maker culture," using off-the-shelf technology to design and fabricate high-tech products that come from your instinctive vision.

  Want to be a better financial planner and get better results for your clients? Trust your gut when you're picking stocks, but also use research and science to design optimal portfolios. The most successful people I know in any business, from publishing to advertising to restaurants, are the ones who balance decisive gut instinct with actions based on facts and research.

MIND FROM WHOM YOU SEEK COUNSEL

You might be thinking, "DeVon, your story is great and I'm really happy for you, but I don't work in Hollywood." This principle works no matter what field your career is in because we're all faced with choices:

- What career path to take out of school

- Whether or not to test a new career path if the current one isn't working out

- Whether or not to ask for a raise or better deal

- Saying "No" to an offer that isn't quite right

- Saying "Yes" to a challenging project or job that might be beyond your current abilities

- Quitting a job to pursue a creative dream like acting or writing

- Quitting a job to start a business

- Relocating for an opportunity

- Taking a flyer on a creative project

No matter how rational the decision to do any of these things might seem, there will always be an element of gut instinct in them. Your instinct could wake you up in the middle of the night with a stunning idea for a new product. It could blindside you one afternoon with the feeling that you're unhappy at your current job and need to leave as soon as possible. It might nudge you into believing that a salary offer that seems fair is really less than what you're worth.

In my experience, when God is working in your gut, the feelings tend to show up in one of two ways:

1. A strong feeling or compulsion, often coming out of nowhere. For example, the sudden, overwhelming desire to go back to college and get your graduate degree.

2. An overpowering sense that a choice you're faced with is either right or wrong.

Another example from author Malcolm Gladwell illustrates the power of such intuition. The Getty Museum in Los Angeles bought an ancient Greek statue called a *kouros* for $10 million after multiple experts certified it as genuine. But then other observers, including an archaeologist, said that they "felt" the statue was not genuine. Their gut instinct spoke so loudly that the museum went against the advice of the experts, tested the statue scientifically, and found that it was indeed a forgery. Score one for gut instinct.

The issue of experts brings up a crucial point about trusting your gut: being mindful of whom you go to for advice and counsel when you want to follow your instincts. When I decided to leave Sony, a number of experienced friends in the business gave me excellent counsel and didn't try to talk me out of it. However, instead of consulting with someone qualified to address our need, we often consult with friends, family members, or people in our church who have no experience with the career issue we're facing. Sometimes, those people will try to talk us out of an idea, especially if it doesn't line up with what they think we should be doing. Remember the idea of putting your talent in a box? This is the same idea: they are trying to contain something that makes them uncomfortable.

But when people try to talk you out of a gut decision that you and they know comes from the Lord, what they're really saying is, *I don't believe that you have what it takes to make this work.* They might not be saying that consciously, and they might be saying it because they really care about you and don't want to see you crash and burn, but it's still an expression of a lack of faith. I try to remember that such people usually mean well, but that they're looking at my gut feeling from a place of fear—fear that I'll fail—and you should never, ever make a decision out of fear.

Be careful who your counselors are. There are other considerations to keep in mind when people offer counsel about your decision:

- Know who they are.

- Determine if they're reliable.

- Investigate their agenda.

Accept counsel from people who have more experience at what you're doing than you do and don't be so quick to worry about their spirituality. If there are practical issues you need guidance on, you need people who can give you good advice even if they might be of a different faith. I've gotten some of the best career advice from colleagues who are different from me in every way. Yet they have experience in the area where I need counsel, and that's valuable to me.

Above all, when you face critical career decisions, seek out advice from someone who is already where you want to be in your career. Suppose you're looking to move into a different area of your industry. Someone who is successful in that area will have more knowledge about how it works and who the players are and might give you guidance that will make all the difference.

Now, before you get up in arms, I'm not saying that you shouldn't seek the guidance of your peers. In certain circumstances, it's okay. Just don't make the peer-to-peer advice the only advice you seek, especially when you're at a crossroads and facing a gut-instinct decision. This is a time when having "virtual mentors" helps because, even if you can't locate someone with experience to talk with directly, you can research how your virtual mentor handled similar situations and glean pertinent information from that.

Exodus

Decisions based on gut instinct can be risky, and they can lead to mistakes such as failed projects and bad deals. They can also lead to huge successes, and smart organizations encourage their people to trust their gut, take some risks, and even court failure if it has the potential to lead to greater things. But if you're constantly coming to your superiors with gut-level ideas and being shot down—if they see risk and failure as something to avoid, not encourage—then it might be time to go somewhere that recognizes the value of gut instinct as much as market data.

FIGHT YOUR FEAR

"For God has not given us the spirit of fear, but of power, and of love, and of a sound mind" (2 Timothy 1:7, KJV). Fear. It's our strongest emotion . . . and the one most likely to prevent you from acting on the gut instinct God is communicating to you. What this boils down to is a tug of war between fear and faith. If you trust that God is guiding you in the right way through your intuition, you're going to do whatever your gut tells you to, without questioning. But people rarely do that because they don't trust, not really.

We don't get enough experience through the church in trusting our intuition, which is strange because intuition and instinct are really the Holy Spirit at work in us. The Holy Spirit is there to guide us and give us knowledge and wisdom. But in order to trust our intuition as a sort of compass for our lives, we first have to trust it for the very first time. Remember Joe Roth? He's completely confident in trusting his gut because he's had experience with it. He acted on it once and it worked out, so he did it again. Most of the time, trusting his instinct has paid off for him, so it's built his confidence. The next time his instinct tells him to try something, he doesn't even hesitate. He figures out what it means and does it.

At some point, you have to step out in faith and say, "Okay God, I'm going to trust this feeling You're giving me. I'm not comfortable doing it, it's scaring me, but I'm going to try it." Hopefully, it works out reasonably well and you say, "That wasn't so bad." You gain confidence. But in the church, we aren't taught how to use our gut instinct—how to listen to it, harness it, use it to fuel your success, and use prayer to interpret it. We pray because we want God's best for our lives. We pray because we really want to understand what we're supposed to do. But no matter how much we plan and analyze, in the end, it comes down to a simple question: do we trust God or don't we?

There were no statistics that could have told me it was the right time for me to leave Sony, no report on faith-based producers that could have given me the final push. I had an intuition based upon my logical assessment of the environment I was in, how I was feeling, and what I wanted to do with my career in the future. That's the ideal state: strong, clear intuition combined with your own internal assessment of a number of factors:

1. How are you feeling?

2. Is that feeling due to the environment that you're in?

3. What other factors are contributing to this feeling?

4. How strongly is your ego involved? Nine times out of ten, if you let your ego guide you, it's going to lead you in the wrong direction.

Should you look at all the information available to you, like salaries, hiring trends, cost of living in other cities, and that sort of thing? Absolutely. Look at all the information that's available to you. Use facts and data to help you determine *how* to follow your gut: when to make your move, what to ask for in a new position, if an offer is fair or not, and so on. But don't let data be what convinces you to say yes or no to your instinct. If you do, more often than not you'll make the wrong choice.

Here's a good process to follow:

1. Trust your gut the first time.

2. See what happens.

3. Learn what you can.

4. Learn to recognize God speaking through your instinct.

5. Trust again.

6. Learn more.

7. Repeat.

Act on your gut instinct once and see what happens. It's like riding a bike: you'll never really learn until you take off the training wheels.

Away from the Workplace

Gut instincts drive choices in every area of life, but I find them to be incredibly powerful in romantic relationships. If you've read *The Wait,* you know that Meagan's and my relationship and marriage were driven by our gut feelings about each other—instincts that we denied, then listened to, and finally followed into our season of celibacy and wonderful discovery. If we hadn't listened to God, we might not be together. For instance, I did NOT want to date an actress. So, who did God tell me my spouse was? An actress! And I can't imagine ever being happier. In relationships, your instincts might draw you to someone who you don't think is right for you—someone who doesn't fit The List you've drawn up. Throw it away and follow your gut. You might be surprised.

SPIRITUAL PRINCIPLES, SECULAR SUCCESS

I've talked a bit about risk and failure, but when it comes to success in the secular world, they bear deeper examination. In the entertainment business, the pattern is persistent: every time Hollywood plays it safe and makes movies based on data and not creative instincts, they turn out junk. Also, every year, it seems like we hear about a handful of visionary filmmakers who defy all the people telling them their idea won't work, get their picture made somehow, and shock the world with a dark-horse hit.

Ever hear of a guy named George Lucas? Of course you have. George is a legend in the business; one of the reasons I wanted to go to the USC School of Cinematic Arts is because he went there. But early on, nobody believed in George. First, nobody wanted his first major release, *American Graffiti;* Fox, Warner, MGM, and Paramount all passed on it. Finally, Universal said yes, and the movie came out in 1973 and made $140 million on a $775,000 budget.

You would think that kind of profit would've gotten George a green light for his next project no matter what it was. Not so fast. In most industries, the trouble with having a hit is that the powers that be want your next thing to be a carbon copy. Originality terrifies people. But George didn't want to make another period piece. He had a two-page outline for a space adventure movie based on shows from his childhood like *Buck Rogers* and *Flash Gordon*. But nobody saw the potential, and United Artists and Universal said no. Twentieth Century Fox finally gave George a shot and he spent two years honing the concept into what became something called *Star Wars*. I trust you've heard of it.

There's something at work here that you've got to remember if you want to listen to God in your gut when you make career decisions:

**Most people don't truly believe something
will happen until it does.**

Even a lot of people of faith do not really believe that God will keep His word and that gut instinct will pay off until after it happens. That's just human nature. We want proof. We don't usually think something *can* happen until it *does* happen. When you step out in faith based on instinct, you should assume that most people won't believe you can succeed. It doesn't make them bad people; it means they've yet to find that place where faith really is the substance of things unseen. You might even be there yourself and that's fine. It's hard to take a risk purely on faith. But ask yourself this: when you look at the people who don't believe something is possible until it happens, how are they doing in their careers? Are they playing it safe and going nowhere? Are they happy? Are they doing work with meaning and purpose—work that serves God?

I'll bet the answer to all three questions is no. If you don't want to be one of those people, perhaps it's time you trusted your gut completely, without hesitation, and let God show you what He can do in your career and your life. Let this be an exercise in deepening your faith. Look back at the times in your life when God has spoken to you. What happened when you listened? What happened when you acted upon it? Are there any missed opportunities you could learn from? What might the next step of faith look like for you?

I want you to do something right now. Put both of your hands on your stomach and listen for what you hear. What do you hear God saying to you as you listen to your gut? Then after you listen, ask God, "What are You calling me to do?" And whatever answer He reveals, know that it will require faith. You've got to believe it before you do it, and then take steps to achieve it even before you know it's going to work. The reason God hides in your gut is because He wants us to become more proficient in exercising faith because faith is the only thing that makes us acceptable to him (Romans 5:1).

USING INSTINCT TO ADVANCE YOUR CAREER

In trying to have a more fulfilling, more financially rewarding career, the best advice I can give you is to listen. Pay attention to gut feelings that pull on you with powerful emotions—compulsions that won't leave you alone. Those are strong signs that God is working to lead you in a new direction.

This is where prayer can be a powerful tool. Prayer quiets the mind so you're not hearing the noise of your thoughts, leaving you open to the whisperings of the Holy Spirit. Prayer helps you determine who is speaking through your intuition, God or you. We all have our own internal voice that's sometimes driven by forces like ego, fear, greed, or envy. How do we determine whether it's God or you? Prayer. If your instinct doesn't have a tinge of fear or those other negative feelings and seems to have sprung into your spirit fully formed, it's God saying, "I have something I think you should do."

I pray for understanding of my gut instincts every day. Should I trust my feelings about the direction of a new TV show? Should I buy this script or that one? Those are instincts driven by experience, but I need to know if I'm coloring my instinct with the desire to copy what some other producer did or to follow some trend. Prayer helps give me clarity, and it will do the same for you. Other tools that will help turn your gut into a powerful career-building resource:

- **When in doubt, take the risk.** It might seem counterintuitive, but you actually risk more by playing it safe than you do by daring to be original. Trusting your gut and taking risks is how you come up with truly original ideas, and those are what make careers. Whether it's an idea for a new product, a business model, a work of art, or a way to save your company money, risk speaking and following it. At the very least, if the idea doesn't pan out, you'll earn respect for your courage.

- **Know your industry.** Read, attend conferences, network, learn every facet. That will help you follow up on your instinct-driven decisions with smart actions. This will also help you know whom you can trust and who has a sketchy track record.

- **Look for signs.** God works in signs and symbols, and when He really wants you to act on a gut feeling, He'll often send signs your way. They might not be neon signs saying, "Take the job," but they could be new people coming into your life, details falling into place perfectly, or strange quirks of timing, like the job you covet at a rival company becoming available just as you're thinking about leaving your current employer. Pay attention to the signs. They're not random.

- **Don't be afraid to upset some people along the way.** In going after what you feel in your gut, there's rarely room for compromise, and that can make some people mad. Sometimes, it's unavoidable. As long as you're straight with everyone and don't torch a relationship deliberately, don't be afraid to ruffle some feathers in following the path God's laid out for you.

- **Live your values.** Your best chance to avoid setting fire to any bridges while you follow your instincts is to adhere to your

Christian values. Be fair and honest. Communicate. Keep your word. Deliver what you promise when you promise. Keep things confidential when asked to. If you have commitments, live up to them before you move on. Care about people. Do those things and no matter what God's voice in your gut tells you to do next, you'll always earn people's respect.

Thou Shalt

» Pay attention to coincidences.
» Look for people in the position you want to be in to be your wise counselors.
» Write down your crazy, high-risk ideas so you don't forget them.
» Have faith that God will lead you where you should go.

Thou Shalt Not

» Look for logic or patterns in instinct. Sometimes there's no rhyme or reason in what God's asking you to do, but that doesn't make it wrong.
» Give the doubters power over you.
» Procrastinate and miss God's window of opportunity.

6

YOU GET WHAT YOU NEGOTIATE (NOT WHAT YOU'RE WORTH)

Let us never negotiate out of fear. But let us never fear to negotiate.
—John F. Kennedy

O ver my twenty years in Hollywood, I've learned a great deal about the importance of being able to negotiate, not just from a business perspective but also from a practical one. During my last contract cycle as an executive, I was negotiating for a contract that would give me:

- The freedom to make different movies for different divisions.

- The ability to specialize in making some faith-based and urban-genre projects while still developing and overseeing more mainstream projects.

- The opportunity to have flexibility in my schedule so I could travel and continue to build my life as a speaker and author.

When it came down to that negotiation, I took the initiative and created a twelve-page PowerPoint presentation that clearly articulated what I wanted to do. I made the presentation to then–Sony Pictures Entertainment chairmen Michael Lynton and Amy Pascal and to Columbia Pictures president Doug Belgrad.

They loved it. They told me that they'd never had an executive come to them with such a clear vision and take the time to lay it out in such a concise manner. They all said, "Let's do it." But here's a lesson in negotiation: *mutual agreement is one thing, sorting out the details is another*. Nobody knew how to structure my deal because they'd never done one like it before. A few days later, they made me an initial offer that was good but didn't give me the flexibility to fully execute everything I had laid out in my proposal. I turned it down. Strike one. They went back to the drawing board and came back with another offer that gave me some of the flexibility, but not the resources to acquire material. I said, "If I accept this offer in this form, how will I execute on everything you want me to execute on?" Strike two.

I'll never forget what happened next. Amy, Michael, Doug, and George Rose, the head of HR, and I got together for a meeting to discuss how to make my deal work. Apparently, I had stumped them. Amy told me, "We have never met this many times and had this many discussions about somebody's job."

We were at an impasse, and that might have scared most people. Maybe I was being too difficult and requiring too much of their time. But I knew that wasn't what she meant. I didn't easily fit into the corporate structure, and what I wanted to do was so uniquely valuable that it required time, consideration, and creative thinking. I loved this. I was challenging the top people at Sony to think differently about me. While that slowed things down, it also meant that they would be invested in me. They understood the value I had created and believed I could create even more; this was why they were thinking about how best to handle me.

Eventually, a deal was made that made both sides happy. The powers that be took me directly out of the Columbia Pictures division so I could make some movies through Columbia and TriStar, gave me development money so I could buy scripts, promoted me to senior vice president, and raised my salary. I effectively had my own pod within the studio.

I was thrilled. Before we closed the deal, I found out that I would be making a little bit less than other senior vice presidents had historically been paid. But I said, "What I've gotten in this deal is more valuable than more money. I've gotten more time, more flexibility, and more freedom." There was no way to put a price on that.

DON'T LET HUMILITY UNDERMINE YOUR VALUE

Through all my various negotiations, I have come to learn the next Commandment:

You Get What You Negotiate (Not What You're Worth)

This is true not only in your professional life but in every area of your life. People may know your worth but life isn't merit based; you can't assume that people are going to give you what you've earned. You must negotiate for it. Many Christians labor under the misconception that being humble and moral and righteous is enough to get you what you want. And that's just not true. We also have to know what it means to be *valued* and *valuable* and bring forth both in how we negotiate. It's essential to have a strong sense of your own self-worth so you can be a fierce advocate for your interests.

As people of faith, we have a hard time assessing our value and then fighting for it. These are not things that we're conditioned to do. While learning scriptures, you never hear the pastor or the elders say, "Here's how you negotiate. Here's what you need to know when you're navigating your career and it comes time to sign a contract. These are the types of alliances you'll need to build. Here's how to realistically assess the value you've created and how you should be compensated for that value." Maybe you are thinking, "Isn't that what business school is for?" But in every career path, not just in Hollywood, and not just in business, we all have to deal with negotiation at some point, whether it's a barista negotiating for a raise, a teacher working to get more supplies for her classroom, or a Realtor trying to get better closing terms for his client. Too many people of faith are ill-equipped to successfully navigate the ins and outs of career advancement, of which negotiation is an essential part.

Why is this especially a problem for people of faith? The problem is our misinterpretation of *humility*. Yes, humility before God is the foundation of our faith—and yes, I believe it when the Bible says, "Humble yourselves, therefore, under God's mighty hand, that he may lift you up in due time " (1 Peter 5:6, NIV) or, "Pride leads to disgrace but with humility comes wisdom" (Proverbs 11:2, NLT). However, we apply these verses in ways that were never intended. What does it mean to be humble? The type of humility the Bible is referencing relates to how we view ourselves relative to God. This type of humility means we should always go low before God, acknowledging that it's His power, mercy, and grace that we need in order to do what He's called us to do. Without these things, we can't be successful. So yes, we should carry ourselves with a humble disposition.

However, that humility isn't code for being a doormat and allowing people or companies to walk all over us. When it comes to negotiating for what you're worth, you can't be overly humble about the value you create. Arrogance has no place in any negotiation, but neither does self-abasement. Never be afraid of articulating your value or being clear about what you want and why you want it. Value who you are, what you know how to do well, and what you bring to the table that nobody else can. Because there's only one person who can do what you do. As you serve, as you learn, and as you apprentice, you become more valuable. You're gaining the experience and expertise you need to finally receive the compensation you've always known you're worth.

One of the ways to walk the tightrope of confident advocacy without crossing into arrogance speaks to the Commandment we learned before:

You Have to Carry a Crown Before You Can Wear One

When you have been of great service and created great value, that becomes your platform for declaring your value and asking for what you want without seeming arrogant. The reason I had such a rapport with the heads of Sony and engaged in such intense, candid negotiation was that I had built up great equity with them. I had worked at Sony for more than six years and worked on some of the studio's biggest and most profitable hits, including *The Pursuit of Happyness, Hancock, 21, The Karate Kid,* and *Jumping the Broom.* If I had tried to make the demands I made without having been of service to the company for years, I would have failed. Having proven myself in performance and character freed me to be assertive while remaining humble.

A SELF-IMAGE OF VALUE

This all starts with a self-image that's based on the knowledge that you create value. Scripture says that we were made in the image of God. Do you realize how powerful that is? God is the most powerful force in the universe and we are made in that same image. We have to get up every day and believe in the person God created who looks back at us in the mirror. If we don't believe in ourselves, we diminish the power by which we were created.

The best way to honor God with our lives is to believe in who He created us to be and live that every day. In addition to being value-based in our beliefs, we must also be value-based in how we view ourselves. You need to believe that you are valuable and keep reminding yourself, "This is who I am. This is what I do well. This is how I'm creating value. This is what I'm worth."

This is where humility—really, *false* humility—sometimes trips us up. Author Jacob Nordby writes, "False humility is a form of psychosis which was imprinted on most of us since birth. It is a mental illness because it locks us in a victim state of keeping our light turned down, denying who we really are and silently begging for permission to simply show up as ourselves in the world. But there is good news. This is a jail whose lock is broken. We can walk free whenever we know the truth, and by so doing we show others an example of an end to madness. An example of freedom." We're taught to be like Jesus—and then we're taught that he was meek and mild, like in the old hymn "Gentle Jesus, Meek and Mild" or the popular Christmas song "Jesus, Oh What a Wonderful Child" with the lyric "Jesus, Jesus, so lowly, meek, and mild."

These representations of Jesus are not historically, biblically, or spiritually accurate. There was nothing meek or mild about how Jesus lived on this earth. He was strategic. He understood the political climate. He was determined. He was focused. He was persistent. He was passionate. All of these things made up who he was, and because of them, he was incredibly effective. Not because of false humility. He walked in the power and authority of his father and he made no excuses for it.

As you are climbing the ladder, bow before God but not before your superiors. Become keenly aware of the value you create. Once you have a sense of that value, and you have tested that value, believe it. Not theologically or intellectually, but practically, because you can see that your work, expertise, and creativity are providing tangible benefits. When I go into the office or when I'm on a set, I know that what I'm doing is valuable. That is empowering. It brings confidence. When you fight for what you know you're worth, bring that confidence. See yourself as a value creator. Research and know how your industry is currently rewarding that value. Once you do that, you'll know what you're worth and what to ask for.

False Idols

Don't lose sight of what you're negotiating for. Yes, you want to be compensated fairly based on the value you create, but there's a spiritual dimension, too. You're working to fulfill part of God's design, and the ultimate purpose of any negotiation is to make you better able to do that. Does that mean more money or a promotion to a better position? It could mean both, but have a clear understanding of what God wants for you and what He intends to do through you if you receive the money or promotion. In the end, you're not just negotiating for yourself. You're negotiating to receive whatever God has ordained for your life to use for His purpose.

THE COMPANY LOOKS OUT FOR ITSELF

Simply asking for what you believe you're worth doesn't mean you will receive it. I've found that many people go into negotiations thinking that the system operates out of fairness and that if they simply present their case, the company, studio, home buyer, or other party will simply say, "Sure, that makes sense."

Sometimes we think, "I'm creating all this value for the company, so they're going to pay me what I'm worth." We assume that the company will do right by us. But it doesn't work like that. The company's first interest is to do right by the company. If the company can do right by the company by doing right by you, that's great, but their number one concern is always to make the best possible deal for the company. If they can get you to settle for a dollar less than you ask for, they will. That doesn't make employers bad people; it's just the nature of business. This is why it's so important to resist the temptation to make negotiations emotional. Because when you feel like the company is doing you wrong, and you get upset about it, it will impair how you negotiate. Keep a level head, understand that this is business, and don't allow your emotions to get the best of you.

I hope understanding that will help you drop any "They're going to give me what I'm worth" illusions. No, they aren't. Any party across the table, whether it's a car dealer, a mortgage broker, or a corporation, will offer you the minimum of what they think you will accept based on their calculation of their desired profit. It's your job to know what you're worth, know what you will accept, and refuse to take less than you're worth.

That is extremely difficult for some people to do, I know. It's difficult even if you weren't raised in the church and taught this idea of false humility. Most of us fear asking for what we want because we're afraid whomever we're negotiating with will say no, and we'll lose the job or opportunity. Too often we don't really value ourselves or what we do enough, so we worry that if we push back in any way, we'll be shown the door. We secretly, subconsciously say to ourselves: *I'm not that valuable, so if I object at all, I'm gone.*

But that's not true. If you're good at what you do, you're valuable. If you're living your Christian values every day, you're valuable. Hard-working people of good character aren't exactly falling off the trees, you know. If you have done your homework and made an educated request for what you believe you're worth based on sound and educated reasoning, the person you're negotiating with may see it differently, but they won't be mad that you had the confidence to ask for what you felt you're worth and backed it up with research. That's what made my assertive negotiations with Sony possible.

Keep something else in mind: the person you're negotiating with will usually offer you less than you're worth *deliberately* to see if you push back. Remember, the organization looks out for its own interest first. That means it's not only okay for you to object to an offer that's below what you're worth, it's *expected*. When you make a confident counteroffer, you'll not only have a better chance to get what you're worth, but also gain respect. Bottom line:

You cannot negotiate from a place of fear.

I wasn't always a confident negotiator. I don't think anyone is. You learn by doing—by pushing back and being bold and finding out that the sky doesn't fall. In fact, even though the person on the other side of the desk from you might bluster and feign outrage when you respond to an offer by asking for more, I've found that to be largely a performance. In my experience, people in authority like when someone has the guts and confidence to demand what they're worth.

How do you gain confidence to do something you've never done? I follow two steps that I recommend to you:

- **Affirm that what you need has already been ordained.** Every morning I read the Word, pray, and then recite my affirmations. Starting in the summer of 2015, one of my affirmations was: "Mainstream television opportunities will maximize my motivational gifts." Then, at the end of the summer of 2016, *The Dr. Oz Show* called and invited me to be a guest on a show they were doing called "Healing America's Grief." The taping went so well that they invited me back multiple times, and now I'm a regular on his show doing segments that Dr. Oz calls "DeVon Interventions." The point is, you don't have to try to "make it" when you understand that God made you. You are already made. Be confident in who God created you to be and what you're called to do, and begin to affirm it every single day.

- **Claim it!** Years ago, when traveling, I would seek out airport bookstores, go over to the bookshelves, touch all the *New York Times* bestsellers, and say, "I claim it in the name of Jesus." I was claiming that I was a *New York Times* bestselling author even before I became one. Eventually, my last book, *The Wait*, became my first *New York Times* bestselling book!

Know that God has greatness in mind for you and don't let that greatness be curtailed by fear. Remember who you are. Keep a confident mindset as a way to fight the fear that wants to creep into your spirit and disrupt your God-ordained success.

THERE'S MORE TO COMPENSATION THAN MONEY

Elizabeth Gabler, president of Fox 2000 Pictures, is one of the most successful, longest-standing studio executives in Hollywood. She's behind such box-office hits as *Hidden Figures, Marley & Me, The Devil Wears Prada, Walk the Line,* and *Cast Away.* She and I had lunch while I was working on this book, and in our conversation, she mentioned she looks at negotiation as more than just getting as much money as you can: it's also about trying to achieve the lifestyle you want.

I agree with her wholeheartedly; when you're facing a negotiation, remember that compensation isn't just about money. Don't get me wrong, money is important, but there are other things that factor into compensation such as time, freedom, and flexibility. It's also about what you value the most and what you feel you need in order to continue to perform on the job. Negotiation isn't just a time when you sit down and discuss your salary and benefits; it's an opportunity to shape your future according to God's vision and your own. So, before you get hung up on pay, don't. Step back and ask, "What do I want my whole life to look like?" We spend so much of our time on the job; it's one of the most important parts of our lives. So why not look at it holistically and try to make work serve not only your financial needs but also your personal ones?

Two more things to think about:

- **Everything comes with a cost.** If you get a $100,000 salary, you're going to have to meet $100,000 worth of expectations. Money costs time. It can cost relationships. Everything you want costs something, so know that if you're pushing the negotiation for the maximum amount of money you can get, that will come with increased expectations and pressure to deliver. These are not bad things, but they are things to be aware of and factor into how you negotiate.

- **What you value will change over time.** When you're twenty-five years old, you might go into a negotiation and want money because you're trying to build your life. You want to buy a house, get a hot car, and travel. Okay. But then you get married and have kids, and you find that, while money is still important, it's not as important as spending time with your little ones. Some types of compensation may matter more, some less. But what you care about will not remain static.

Ask yourself, what kind of compensation would make a difference in your life? Maybe you're a corporate sales rep who spends all her time on the road, and you would love to be able to make some of your sales calls via videoconference. That's a subject for negotiation. Maybe you're a parent and you want to make it home early enough to have dinner with your kids. There are no right answers. There's only what you define as compensation and if you can successfully negotiate for it.

WHAT ARE YOU WORTH?

Star Wars is one of the most successful franchises in the history of the movie business, and part of its legend includes the fact that George Lucas, its creator, negotiated what *Vanity Fair* has called "the best business deal in Hollywood history." The original deal for *Star Wars* was negotiated in 1973–1974 and Lucas's then-attorney, Tom Pollock, explained in an interview with Deadline.com that nobody really wanted this sci-fi adventure. So, when Fox entered into nego-tiations with Lucas, they didn't care about *Star Wars*. As far as they were concerned, Pollock explains, Fox was willing to foot the bill for Lucas's space opera so that they could have his next *American Graffiti* project.

After the success of *American Graffiti,* Lucas could have negotiated for a big pay raise on *Star Wars*. But he chose not to. Why? Because he knew what he was worth. Pollock says Lucas went into the boardroom with two nonnegotiable requests: he wanted to be in charge of the sequels for the films, and he wanted to control all merchandising for *Star Wars*. Pollock said, "It's important to remember that none of the original deal came out of money as those who know something about it might think. It came because George just wanted to be able to make the movies he wanted to make."

Those two decisions, based on understanding his worth, made Lucas a billionaire, because *Star Wars* is one of the most valuable merchandising properties on the planet, with products ranging from action figures to extended universe novels to video games and every-thing in between. In 2012, Lucas closed another deal that *Wired* called "The deal of the century" when he sold his company, Lucasfilm, to Disney for $4 billion.

All of this comes down to a simple question: *what do you believe you are worth?* Beliefs are like the operating system of the mind; they run everything. So, it doesn't matter what I say, what anyone tells you, or even what your research says you should be paid for the value you're creating if you don't *believe* you're worth it. You won't be pro-active in negotiations and you won't make a counteroffer and ask for more; you'll take what they give you with a "Well, at least I still have a job" mentality.

I want more than that for you. God wants more than that for you.

That's why believing in your worth begins with God. God created you to have an exciting destiny and to play a role in His design for the world. He wouldn't have done that if He didn't see great potential in you—if He didn't *value* you. He knows your worth, and He wants you to appreciate it, believe it, and fight for it. If you're not sure, pray. Pray for insight into how God sees you—to see yourself, just for a moment, through God's eyes. You'll see something very different from the person you see now! You'll see a child of God created in God's image, created to be great and to have an impact on this world. If God values you like that, doesn't it make sense to value yourself in the same way?

Now, I know that might not be enough to stoke your sense of your own value, so try this. Now is the time to take it (like the song says) "All the Way Up" in your career. Aspire to things beyond even the goals you've already set. Resolve not to accept less than you are worth, ever. If you accept less, you can begin to feel that you're worth less—*worthless*. When you accept less than your value, you don't just damage yourself in the short-term. You also damage yourself in the long-term because you will subconsciously resent feeling stuck doing a lesser job for lesser pay. This can affect your performance and even lead to a career slowdown.

There's a sort of urban legend that nicely illustrates what I'm talking about, inspired by experiments of a behavioral psychologist named G. R. Stephenson. A group of scientists placed five monkeys in a cage, and in the middle was a ladder with bananas on top. Every time a monkey climbed the ladder to get the bananas, the scientists would blast the rest of the monkeys with freezing water. After a while, every time a monkey started up the ladder, the rest would pull it down and savagely beat it. Then the scientists started bringing in new monkeys, each of which naturally tried to climb the ladder and were beaten. Eventually, a culture developed among the monkeys, even the ones that had never been sprayed with water, that "you just don't try climbing the ladder." The monkeys had been socially conditioned for defeat.

When you begin to work for less than your value, it erodes your sense of self-confidence. You begin to live in a "less-than" way. You deny your destiny. You say, "I'm just happy to have a job. Maybe I was crazy to believe in something big, anyway." You lessen your belief so you can justify lowering your expectations, which mitigates your disappointment at not aspiring to more. It's a dangerous, slippery slope.

When you first come into an industry, you're full of aspirations. You're going to do this and become that. Then reality hits, things become hard, and you begin to question: "Is it possible? Am I capable? Can I do this?" You lower your sights so you can simply get through, day-to-day. The tragedy comes when you look at yourself twenty years from now, and you haven't done any of what God called you to do because you allowed yourself to settle into a long-term state of less-than.

Instead of living with that reality, we psychologically reset our sense of what we're worth so we can be happy at the current level of value that we're getting compensated for, even though we know, deep down, that we're really not at peace.

Don't allow yourself to fall into that habit, because it's hard to escape. Don't allow yourself to get stuck in a role or position that you didn't negotiate for but are now expected to fulfill just because you didn't speak up when it was time. You can make a change and you can make it now; your future depends on it.

Exodus

There are plenty of negotiation scenarios in which you're justified in heading for the exits at your current employer. If they refuse to negotiate on anything but say "Take it or leave it"—walk. If they won't negotiate in good faith (offering you something and then refusing to deliver), run fast. Unfortunately, there are some organizations who want compliant employees who meekly take what they're given. Don't let that be you. You're worth more and deserve better.

TAKE PRIDE IN SERVICE

As believers, we're often wary of *pride*. After all, scripture does say, "Pride goes before destruction, a haughty spirit before a fall. Better to be lowly in spirit along with the oppressed than to share plunder with the proud" (Proverbs 16:18–19, NIV). Does that mean that God doesn't want us to take pride in what we do and ask for what we're worth? Or does it mean that if we do take pride in the value we create, we're setting ourselves up for destruction?

Neither. God doesn't deal in contradictions. If He says that He wants you to go vertical and rise to the highest level you can, that's what He means. The type of pride referenced in scripture refers to arrogance and believing in our own power that is independent of God's power that operates through us. When we begin to believe our own hype, praise ourselves, and think that it was only by our power that we have succeeded, we have become prideful. It's this type of pride that leads to our downfall.

The Bible isn't talking about the type of pride that comes from feeling valuable and having self-respect. Those are positive feelings that you need to excel in work and life. You should feel good about the work you do and in turn feel good about yourself because of that work.

When I worked on *Miracles from Heaven,* by framing my pride in my work as pride in the *service* my work delivered for myself and others, I was able to appreciate success without crossing over into vanity and egotism. You can do the same. If you're a teacher, you can take pride in the grades your students achieve under your tutelage, in the lives you touch, and the kids you send to a brighter future. If you're managing a retail store, you can appreciate the strong sales you're generating and take pride in the relationships you've built over the years with your customers.

There is nothing sinful about pride that comes from a job well done. It's all about what you take pride *in.* Be proud of who you are and whom you are serving, stand on that, and feel good.

Away from the Workplace

As unromantic as it sounds, marriage can be about negotiation, too. Sometimes the reason you're not happy is because you haven't properly negotiated your arrangement with your partner. For instance, maybe you don't mind vacuuming and sweeping, but you're stuck with doing dishes and laundry, which you hate. Because you haven't actually negotiated your marriage, you're stuck doing things that don't bring you value and don't make you feel valued. In a marriage, it's important to keep valuing yourself as an individual because that's the only way you'll speak up for what you want. If you want to have a happy marriage—or if you're with someone you might WANT to marry—don't be afraid to renegotiate. Practice it now. Have an idea of what you want and what the other person wants so you can find a way for both of you to get part of what you want and still feel happy.

HOW TO NEGOTIATE LIKE A BOSS

After you do all that, you've got to come to the negotiating table armed with hard facts. You need to know what your work is worth—how much value you've created and what it means to the people you're negotiating with. Let's talk about how.

- **Know your industry.** Read. Attend events. Find mentors. Do work at every level, even if it seems menial. Figure out what creates real value in your field:
  - Where are the value points in your work?
  - Where are the seams?
  - What are you doing better than anyone else?
  - In what way are you irreplaceable?

- **Look at the data.** Has productivity increased since you came on board? Have costs gone down? Has turnover decreased? Has your division closed more deals? Translate those facts into financial impact, and use that as the baseline for assessing the value you are creating at the place in which you're working.

- **Know what you want before you sit down to negotiate.** However, that doesn't mean only having one goal in mind. That doesn't leave you any room to maneuver. If you ask for something and the other guy says, "No," you don't want to be sitting there with your mouth open and no idea what to do next. Always have a Plan B and even a Plan C. If they knock you down on salary, can you get more vacation time or a better title? If you're closing a sale and the customer won't pay your price, can you get them to sign a long-term sales contract? And so on. Prepare all this in advance, assume you're going to get pushback, and plan for it.

In fact, pushback is a good thing. If you know what your value is and you're really fighting for it, you should expect pushback. If you're not getting it, then that's a sign you're not asking for enough! That's why agents and attorneys always go high with their first ask; they know the other person will push back. But the stage has been set for them to get what they need to get for their client. Resistance, in this context, is a positive sign.

- **Have a good supporting team.** In all my negotiations, I've always had a good team around me to help and give me advice. I'm the quarterback, but my lawyer and agent do the negotiating. In some instances, you will need to find a good attorney who can represent your interests and handle negotiations for you. However, if you are doing the negotiation yourself, don't go into any negotiation unprepared. If you have not sought the counsel of somebody at a higher level than you who has already negotiated a deal like the one you're heading toward, you'll be going into a negotiation unprepared—and that means you're preparing to lose, not win.

- **Be ready to be tough.** You have to be fearless. As the Bob Sugar character said in the film *Jerry Maguire,* "It's not show friends, it's show business." So, prepare. Rehearse. Know what you're going to say, and don't back down until you get a deal that you can feel good about.

- **Benefit everyone.** Remember when I said that any organization is always going to look out for its own interests first, not yours?

That's true, but what happens when you align your interests and theirs? I'll tell you: *you win*. If you want to be a smart negotiator, show clearly how you getting what you want will benefit the people you're negotiating with. You get more money, but they get your big ideas, longer hours, your departmental reorganization plan, your killer app idea—you get the picture. Talk about how your success is their success. That's a winning pitch.

- **Silence is golden.** Don't talk to fill the quiet. When you've said your piece, sit quietly and wait for the other party to respond. Silence can be a powerful negotiating and sales tool because it forces everyone to really think about what's just been said and what will be said next. Get comfortable with that. Once you're done, you're done. It's up to the other party to go next.

- **Don't negotiate with yourself.** Once you've made an offer, don't budge from it until you get a counteroffer. Sometimes, people will ask for something and then, when they don't get a quick yes, immediately start backtracking: "Oh, well, I could actually get by with $5,000 less." Don't do that. Be confident. If you've done your homework, created value, and have sound reasons for what you've asked for, stick to it.

- **Be willing to walk away.** This is the strongest tool in all of negotiating. If you're willing to walk away from a deal or a job if you don't get what you need, you will have the greatest leverage. Walking away tells the other party that you're not needy and will not accept less than you're worth. This is a brave move and should only be used when you can live with the reality of leaving your job.

- **Don't be afraid of no.** Don't second-guess yourself. I find it amazing what people will agree to if you just ask, so ask. Remember, the worst they can do is say no. Don't be afraid of no.

THOU SHALT

- » Understand that your value comes from God and that you are worth a great deal.
- » Ask.
- » Dress the part for in-person negotiations. Be on time and look sharp.
- » Know what you want, including intangibles, and have a floor that you won't go below, ever.

THOU SHALT NOT

- » Apologize for your work.
- » Believe any promises that aren't in writing.
- » Forget to pray before you sit down to negotiate.

7

YOU MUST MASTER
THE WALK OF FAME

And what do you benefit if you gain the whole
world but lose your own soul?
—Jesus (Mark 8:36, NLT)

I don't think I realized that the cost of fame is that
it's open season on every moment of your life.
—Julia Roberts

The quintessential experience for tourists visiting Los Angeles is the Hollywood Walk of Fame. More than ten million tourists from around the world come to visit the 1.3-mile stretch of Hollywood Boulevard where they can see over 2,600 terrazzo and brass stars embedded in the sidewalks. Each star bears the name of a musician, director, actor, producer, or radio or television personality, and in a few cases, a fictional character. The stars are permanent monuments to each honoree's entertainment industry achievements, and given Hollywood's cultural impact, it's no surprise that people from around the world put "visit the Walk of Fame" on their bucket list.

But exactly what is it about fame and the famous that seems to captivate us? From TV shows like *Dancing with the Stars* to *Love and Hip-Hop*, from supermarket magazines like *Us Weekly* to *People*, from blogs like Perezhilton.com to TMZ.com—we live in a fame-obsessed culture. According to Yalda T. Uhls, Ph.D., a senior researcher at the UCLA Children's Digital Media Center whom I worked with when I was an executive at MGM, "Our focus groups have shown that young people are aspiring to fame more than anything else." Jean M. Twenge, Ph.D., coauthor of *The Narcissism Epidemic*, said in an interview with *Teen Vogue*, "The desire to be famous is connected to unhappiness. Research has shown that people who value money, fame, and image are more likely to be anxious and depressed."

Fame doesn't have to mean being a celebrity or walking the red carpet at a Hollywood movie premiere. Fame is being known or talked about by many people, especially because of your notable achievements. By this definition, you can become famous at school, at your job, or in the church where you serve. When you excel at what you do, some measure of fame is inevitable. We've been discussing how to achieve the success that God has specifically called you to, and we'll look here at how to handle it when that success comes your way. But as powerful as success and fame can be, the unchecked, unmanaged desire for and pursuit of them can be as destructive as it is powerful.

When the issue of fame comes up in the church, pastors or elders will often point to the scripture, "And what do you benefit if you gain the whole world but lose your own soul?" (Mark 8:36, NLT). While this is an important question that can help keep our ambition in check, this scripture in and of itself doesn't address how to navigate the notoriety that can come from using our God-given gifts. That's what led me to write this Commandment:

You Must Master the Walk of Fame

In developing your strategy for attaining God-ordained secular success, you must understand that true success is not only something you attain but something you must *manage*. Too often, people talk about "getting to the top" as though once they arrive at a certain position or level of income, all the work is done and they can coast. But that's far from the truth. Arriving at the top means the work is just beginning; it's just different work. Before, you had to strive and struggle to achieve success and recognition; now you have to manage its effect on you and the people around you.

History is filled with examples of people who were able to achieve success but unable to maintain it, and one of the biggest reasons is because of the pressures and seductions of notoriety or fame. When you achieve notoriety and start to get praise from others, it becomes easy to allow the fame to become what motivates your career and life decisions. In the process, you can damage not only your life and career but your soul as well.

THE WALK OF FAME

What is the Walk of Fame? It's a mental framework on how you learn to deal with the notoriety that comes from success. News flash: it's not easy. Look at the headlines and you'll see stories of famous people having difficulties with fame and its rewards. It's easy to be judgmental and critical of them. However, it's much harder than you think to navigate your gift and the notoriety that can come from it.

Fame is being known for your achievements. So, fame is relative. You don't have to be world famous to be famous among your peers or famous in your field. If you are gifted (which you are) and if you're using your God-given talents to excel (which you are), you will be sought out and acknowledged, making some degree of fame a by-product of your success.

My wife, Meagan, understands the seductive nature of fame. She began acting at the age of four, has been in countless movies and TV shows, and has millions of fans around the world. When she got into acting, fame was the furthest thing from her mind. As a youth, she was awkward and wasn't good at sports, so drama was where she found her peace. She kept pursuing it because she loved it and it brought her the most joy. Never did she imagine that developing her God-given gift to act would result in her becoming famous. As she's learned to navigate her own Walk of Fame, she's had to step over many challenges along the way. Some were professional challenges, but others were emotional and spiritual, because no one tells you how to handle fame when it comes.

One of the most important things Meagan has said to me about handling the Walk of Fame is, "Make sure your desire to do what you're aspiring to do is about more than getting fame and being a celebrity." There's a reason for that, and it's one we already unpacked: *everything has a cost*. Fame comes with a cost, too. Once you go through that door, there's no going back. You can't uncheck the fame box once it's checked. I don't say this to scare you but to prepare you. This is why it's important to search the depths of your heart and be honest with yourself about your true motivation for pursuing achievement and acclaim. Are you doing it because you want to be all God created you to be and serve His purpose? Or do you secretly covet praise and flattery?

If you find that you covet fame, I urge you to go before God and ask him to purify your heart. Fix your focus on your purpose and becoming all you were created to be, and then surrender to the process required to fulfill your purpose. Pursue your purpose with your body, mind, heart, and soul and be content with whatever fame comes with that. Do not make fame or notoriety the object of your pursuit.

Learning to master the walk means learning to master the power that comes from fame. Pray, pray, and pray some more that God will prepare your heart, mind, and soul to walk well when success and then fame comes. Fame is power and generates power, and if you're unprepared for it, it can rock you to your core. Fame is seductive. It gives you the ability to get things done. It opens doors of opportunity that appear closed to others. It can influence hearts and minds. There's a famous line from *Spider-Man:* "With great power comes great responsibility." Well, with great fame also comes great responsibility, because fame gives you the power to lead people closer to a virtuous life or further away from it. Years ago, basketball legend and current TNT host Charles Barkley made headlines when he said, "I'm not a role model." He was wrong. Whether he wanted that responsibility or not, when you become famous you do model a role that others will be compelled to emulate—good or bad.

Walking the Walk of Fame well means staying grounded, and that takes humility. Humility reminds us that we didn't give ourselves the gifts we have. Even when we feel good about the hard work we've done to become successful, humility helps us avoid taking such pride in the outcome that our ego gets puffed up. We're all vulnerable to the temptations of the ego: feelings of superiority, thinking the rules don't apply to us, thinking we can "phone it in" and still come out on top because we're so awesome, to name a few. Reminding ourselves that everything we have is in part the result of an incredible divine gift is a wonderful way to stay humble and avoid the traps that can come with success.

In striving for enduring humility, it's critical to keep people around you who will tell you the truth. When you become successful, you will encounter people who want things from you. To get what they want, they won't tell you the truth, but a version of the truth they think you want to hear. This is actually harmful because your greatest asset to fame management is *reality*. Fame can create an alternate reality that causes you to lose touch with who you are and what really matters. I've come across many famous people who surround themselves with "yes men" who tell them what they want to hear—even at the expense of their own well-being. As you make your way to the top, keep people in your life who will keep you honest.

Even LeBron James, one of the most famous people on the planet, acknowledges the importance of good people. He once said, "You know, my family and friends have never been yes-men: 'Yes, you're doing the right thing, you're always right.' No, they tell me when I'm wrong, and that's why I've been able to stay who I am and stay humble."

GIVE PRAISE WHERE PRAISE IS DUE

At the heart of the matter is the question of *praise*. To illustrate, let's go back to the story of the Hebrew Boys in the book of Daniel. In Chapter three, King Nebuchadnezzar decided to make a golden ninety-foot statue and commanded everyone in Babylon to fall down and worship the golden image when they heard the music play. He threatened anyone who didn't obey with death in the fiery furnace. Shadrach, Meshach, and Abednego refused, and, furious, the king brought the Hebrew Boys before him and told them that if they didn't obey, he would order them killed.

What upset the king so much? It was a conflict about praise. Praise is an expression of approval or admiration or both for someone or something. In this story, there was a conflict over who was going to get the admiration, the king or the God of the Hebrew Boys. The king's narcissistic need to be the object of praise—of worship, really—fueled his appetite for validation so much that he wasted vital resources building a golden statue for no other purpose than to convince others (and himself) of his power. He wanted to be worshiped like a god, yet he didn't understand that worship is only for God. Rick Warren, author of the blockbuster bestseller *The Purpose Driven Life,* has a definition of worship that I've always liked: honoring God with our lifestyle. The Hebrew Boys refused to bow down because they realized the truth:

We were created to give praise, not receive it.

They knew the only one worthy of their praise and worship was God—not the king, and definitely not a golden statue. And they also understood that bowing down to the statue would indicate a dangerous lifestyle shift. It would communicate the message that they were more comfortable living a life of conformity that valued worshiping the king over worshiping their God.

The battle for praise cuts to the very heart of the war between good and evil. Look at the Devil. The events that led to the Fall and the Devil (a.k.a. Lucifer) becoming Lord of Lies revolved around the fact that he wanted to be the one who received the praise, not God (King Nebuchadnezzar was guilty of the same transgression). What was the result? Banishment from Heaven and being cast to earth along with a third of the angels who were foolish enough to harbor the same idea. The eternal battle between good and evil began with this question: *Will you receive praise or give it?* It continues today, fought in the hearts and spirits of each one of us.

One of the most popular psalms is Psalm 150, which reads in

verse 6 (NIV), "Let everything that has breath praise the LORD. Praise the LORD." The Bible also says that God has angels encamped around Him that offer Him continuous praise and that we were created with the disposition to offer praise to Him from Whom we came. Adam and Eve, Moses, David, Jesus—all the figures that God used in the Bible— when they were at their most successful, were acknowledging and appreciating the role God played in their lives. They also resisted the temptation to build an altar to their own greatness; instead, they were humble and grateful to Him. When they weren't? Well, look at Samson.

Giving praise is part of our divine design. We can give praise in two forms: praise to God and praise to others in the form of encouragement. Have you ever been depressed but given someone an encouraging word and found your spirits lifted? That's because you were created to give praise. It feels good. We don't have to teach our bodies to appreciate a drink of cool, clear water; when we're thirsty, drinking water feels great because we need it to survive. We thrive on it. Praise is water for our spirit. The more we give, the more refreshed we feel.

Exodus

Prioritize praising God and not accepting praise for yourself. However, that does not mean you should allow someone else to take credit for what you do. Unfortunately, many lines of work are rife with this sort of thing: people trying to take credit for the work and ideas of others. God asks for humility but not cowardice. Be observant and diligent about making sure that, if you do terrific work, you get the credit for it. If you're in a field or company where someone else is always trying to climb the ladder by standing on your back, it's time to move on.

PRAISE IS MORE THAN AN UPBEAT SONG

In church, we often express praise to God through worshiping to upbeat music. Every church service I've ever been to has a time for "praise and worship." That's when the praise team gets up and sings songs before the minister preaches. Traditionally, the up-tempo songs are considered "praise" while the slow or moderate tempo songs are "worship." These songs can be a great way for us to express our praise to God, but praise is more complex than just the tempo of a song.

First of all, praise to God is definitely not about flattery. It's admiration. It's gratitude. It's acknowledgment. Praise is outward-facing appreciation. Instead of directing appreciation inward (toward the self) we direct it outward (toward God) as a way to recognize that we are not the source of our gifts and talents. You did not come into this world of your own accord. You did not give yourself the desires or the gifts you have. Neither did I. Why do I have a burning desire to inspire people through entertainment? Because God gave me that desire and the ability to do it came from Him as well. A voice like Adele's isn't just a matter of training. It's a gift endowed to her as part of her creation. The discerning eye of a graphic designer or the sharp palette of a restaurant chef? All are innate abilities that come to them from God. If we acknowledge this as truth, we also must acknowledge that every gift has a Giver. So, when we say "thank you" for our gifts and talents, we are appreciating God, the Giver of every good and perfect gift.

Second, praise is also about encouraging others. This is one of the most powerful things we can do to become who God calls us to be. Think about the structure of the word: *en-courage*. It literally means to give people courage and help them overcome fear! That is powerful! Learn the practice of encouraging others. Sometimes people feel so insecure that they fear giving praise to a colleague, a friend, or a family member because it will diminish their own accomplishments. The most successful people I know are the most generous with encouragement. If you find yourself falling into this trap, pray that God will show you how valuable you are, and then express that value by extending praise to others.

Don't be so focused on your own well-being and career pursuits that you don't take time to look left and right and see who might need an encouraging word. No matter what stage of life we are in, we all have the power to encourage someone else. The pursuit of success is tough and filled with highs and lows. When you take the time to encourage someone in their journey, you have no idea how much you might be helping them make it for one more critical day.

My life and career have been beneficiaries of this type of praise. One day, when I was an executive at Sony, I was feeling low because I felt like none of my dreams were ever going to come true. I was in the office of one of my bosses, Ange Giannetti, executive vice president of Columbia Pictures, trying not to show how depressed I was feeling. As we were discussing our projects, she stopped and said, "What's wrong with you, honey?" I was shocked that she could see right through me. So, I said, "I feel stuck, and I'm afraid I'm never going to make it." She looked at me and said, "Honey, you're gonna be just fine. You keep showing up and doing what you're doing, it's only a matter of time."

This brings tears to my eyes even as I reflect on it now. She didn't have to be concerned about me at all, yet she chose to take the time to encourage me when I needed it the most. That's the power of praise.

THE DANGERS OF PRAISE ADDICTION

We are all in search of validation. We want to know that we are accepted, on the right path, and doing a good job. There's nothing wrong with needing positive reinforcement as a means to feel good and encourage us to keep going. However, be mindful that while positive reinforcement can be an asset, it can also become a liability when it affects your *internalization* or *intention*.

The *Cambridge Dictionary* defines *internalize* as "to accept an idea, attitude, belief, etc., so that it becomes part of your character." John Wooden, the legendary UCLA men's basketball coach who led UCLA to a record ten NCAA championships in a twelve-year period—including seven titles in a row—knew the dangers of internalization. He said, "You can't let praise or criticism get to you. It's a weakness to get caught up in either one."

When you internalize praise, you begin to base your self-worth on it. But our true value comes from within, not from without. So, when we base our self-worth on other people's opinions of us, we set ourselves up for failure. We start to seek the opinions of others to validate ourselves, which is the equivalent of building a house on sand: it cannot and will not stand. *Praise is an unstable master.* Opinions shift like sand, and if your sense of your own value is based on these opinions, it will be as changeable and fragile as a house built on sand.

Previously, we learned about negotiating from a place of strength blended with humility, and that comes into play here, too. Be careful not to turn negotiations into forums in which you seek praise for praise's sake.

There is no external force that can validate who you already are. True self-worth comes from believing that the fact of your birth is all the validation you need. Positive reinforcement doesn't validate you; it's just a sign of the validation you already possess. When you understand this, it then gives you a context for the praise you receive. You will be able to resist internalizing praise to the point that *not* receiving it affects your self-worth.

What about intention? Intention is the reason we do what we do and the goal we hope to reach in doing it. As you are pursuing your goals, be mindful of your intentions and try to keep them pure. You've heard the adage, "The road to hell is paved with good intentions"? It persists because we often have intentions that start out as honorable but become corrupted and end up in a different place entirely. Frequently, this happens because praise from others becomes our only measure of success. If receiving praise becomes the reason you do what you do, your intention shifts from purpose to praise. Instead of pursuing things that are purposeful in your life, you begin to focus on the activities that bring you notoriety and adulation.

The difference between the two is monumental. As we've discussed, when artists try to please their audience (praise) instead of focusing on their gift (purpose) they tend to make the wrong choices. Actor Orlando Bloom (*Pirates of the Caribbean*) says, "As an actor, you can't think about the end result or the fame; you just have to focus on the day you're in. You have no control over the finished product or what people think of it, so all you have is the experience of making it, and you have to stay focused on that."

Pursuing praise is addictive. You begin to change everything you do in order to get another hit of praise, then another. Each bit of praise you get—a great performance review, a pat on the back from a superior, a positive review of your record or short story, likes on Instagram—gives you a small hit of the drug called validation. But that empty validation doesn't last. Marilyn Monroe echoed this sentiment when she said, "Fame doesn't fulfill you. It warms you a bit, but the warmth is temporary."

When getting praise becomes your intention, you can compromise everything you stand for until your life and relationships are irrevocably changed. I've seen it happen. When you're addicted to praise, you'll outsource your peace to people or situations that can never fulfill you.

WHO IS YOUR GOD?

The upshot of this is to be cautious about whom you make into your God—whom you give your praise to. For example, in Hollywood and elsewhere, people sometimes make their bosses their God. I've seen people who work for CEOs, celebrities, and even ministers treat these people like God and worship at the altar of their "throne." They will do anything their bosses ask, even if it defies their values. But bosses are not God, and treating them as such can undermine you. When you give more praise to people in power than you do to God, you will become fearful and tentative because you will believe that your fate is in their hands—not God's. You'll think, "If I don't do everything this person asks, I'm not going to have a job."

That is not the case. God's purpose determines your opportunities, not the decisions of whom you work for. Resist the temptation to praise the person who signs your paycheck. When you honor God as the true boss in your life, He will handle any earthly boss who would ask you to do something that would violate who you are. He is a God of infinite possibilities. We serve a God rich in houses and lands. If your boss decides that you're not a good fit, so what? No boss determines your worth in God's eyes. In a heartbeat, He can bring you a new opportunity that makes the old one pale in comparison.

Remember the Hebrew Boys? Even after the king threatened them with death, they refused to praise him. King Nebuchadnezzar threw them in the fire and turned it seven times hotter. However, the boys did not die. In fact, the king saw what looked like an angel in the fire with them. He brought them out of the fire and he shouted, "Praise be to the God of Shadrach, Meshach and Abednego . . . they . . . were willing to give up their lives rather than worship any god except their own God . . ." (Daniel 3:28, NLT). After this incident, the king not only rescinded his death sentence but gave them a promotion. You will see God show up in your life when you honor Him even above the people you work for.

Don't mistake me; the people you work for can all play vital roles in your happiness and success, and you should respect them and express your gratitude to them as often as you can. Just don't praise them as the source of all that you have. They're contributors, but only God is the source. Thank those who deserve it but give praise only to the One who has given you everything.

THE SPOTLIGHT SHINES, BUT IT ALSO BURNS

Consider this analogy. When you spend a little time in the sun, it feels wonderful. It warms your skin, lends you a tanned, healthy glow, and even improves your health. Basking in the sunshine for half an hour on a spring day is a pure pleasure. So, let's acknowledge the good feeling that comes from fame. It feels good to be known and for people to know and like what we do. It's a nice feeling when people come up to me and say they liked one of my movies or they are fans of my wife's work. It's a good indicator of the impact I'm having on the world, and, just like basking in the sunshine for a little while, it gives me a warm feeling.

But what happens when you spend hours out baking in the sun? Pleasure turns into agony. You get a serious sunburn. Even worse, too much exposure can cause the UV light to damage your skin cells and even lead to skin cancer. It's not meant to be a subtle metaphor. That's what happens when you soak up too much praise. Too much praise gets into your bones, your cells, your entire body—becomes the reason *why* you do what you do. When that happens, you can get utterly lost.

Tiger Woods was once considered the greatest golfer in the world. He won fourteen major tournaments in eleven years, and *Forbes* named him the first athlete to earn $1 billion. At one point, he was bringing in more than $100 million annually in endorsement deals. However, on November 26, 2009, his world would change forever. His then-wife, Elin Nordegren, discovered he had been cheating with another woman—but that was just the beginning. As the story unfolded, multiple women from all over the world came forward to confess they had been with Tiger while he was married. Tiger ended up losing his marriage, his reputation, and his endorsement deals with Nike, Gillette, Accenture, and Gatorade, to name a few. The turmoil also cost him the game he loved and mastered from such an early age; he has not won a major tournament since the story broke. When asked about how all this could have happened, he responded, "Money and fame made me believe I was entitled. I was wrong and foolish."

False Idols

A trap that's easy to fall into is only praising God when life is easy. The fact is, life won't always go smoothly, but that doesn't mean it's not filled with reasons to express gratitude to the One who made you. First of all, praise God for simply being alive, having the chance to pursue success, and for giving you the purpose that gets you out of bed every day. Praise that only happens when things go right is empty praise. Remember to ". . . give thanks in all circumstances; for this is God's will for you in Christ Jesus" (1 Thessalonians 5:18, NIV). Keep getting up each day, putting your best foot forward, trusting that ". . . for those who love God all things work together for good . . ." (Romans 8:28, ESV).

WALK IT OUT

As we've seen from many, many people who have been laid low by the pursuit of fame, saying, "Give praise to God" isn't enough by itself to keep you on track when you're in hot pursuit of your career goals. Scandals, corruption, public humiliations, broken lives, and failed marriages all confirm that the pursuit of fame is seductive, even for people with a strong foundation in their faith. It's all too easy to walk out of church with every intention of giving praise to God and climbing the ladder with a grateful heart, only to jump into the lion's den on Monday morning and forget all of the weekend's lessons.

As we learn to master the Walk of Fame, here are five strides that can help us keep our bearings and retain our humility and perspective:

1. **Remember why you're doing what you're doing.** What is the purpose of your work and your pursuit of achievement? Are you still in touch with what got you started to begin with? What did you want to accomplish in the world when you started? Through all the ups and downs I've faced in my career, I've always worked hard to keep my intention front and center: I exist to motivate people with the urge, information, or ability to do something positive in their life. That's my *why*. What's yours?

2. **Remember what it's all for.** Are you chasing success for God's glory or your own? Who are you serving with what you're doing? What you're doing is bigger than you. You have no idea how many people are connected to your pursuit of purpose. The impact you are having far exceeds what you can even com-

prehend right now, so keep walking in discipline, commitment, and integrity. It *will* pay off.

3. **Remember who's watching**. Whether it's for someone you know or someone you will never meet, you are a role model. Right now, someone is watching you and evaluating how you adhere to your convictions in a world of moral ambiguity and short-cuts. Actions don't just speak louder than words—they scream! Do a check for hypocrisy in your life—are you saying one thing to the people watching and doing another when they've left?

4. **Remember your vision.** When you started out on this journey to career achievement, how did you see yourself living when you achieved your dream? Keep this vision of your life in the front of your mind. This vision will act as a GPS system; whenever you get frustrated, check in with it. Before any movie comes out, studios will release a trailer to advertise what the movie is about and when it's being released. The vision you have in your mind is the trailer for your life. Keep playing it over and over again. It will come to pass.

5. **Remember, you have limited time.** This quote from Steve Jobs reminds us to get about God's purpose and not waste time: "Remembering that I'll be dead soon is the most important tool I've ever encountered to help me make big choices in life. Because almost everything—all external expectations, all pride, all fear of embarrassment or failure—these things just fall away in the face of death, leaving only what is truly important. Remembering that you are going to die is the best way I know to avoid the trap of thinking you have something to lose. You are already

naked. There is no reason not to follow your heart." Keep in mind that your time is limited, and you will be able to use it more effectively toward your purpose.

I recommend checking these strides weekly, more often if needed. It's a powerful, simple, and emotionally potent tool for maintaining perspective.

Away from the Workplace

If you're a parent, you know that one of life's great pleasures is watching your children excel. It fills up your spirit. But there are parents who seem to think that their children's success is important because of what it says about *them*. Don't fall into that trap. Your children may be a living testament to what a great mom or dad you've been, but that's for other people to decide. Let your kids have the spotlight and take private pride in knowing the important role you played.

SPIRITUAL PRINCIPLES, SECULAR SUCCESS

One of the secrets I have found to be most helpful in mastering the Walk of Fame is simply watching role models who are doing it the right way. Pick out individuals from any field—it doesn't have to be your own—who are successful and yet somehow bring a sense of humility and gratitude to everything they do. This is another way you can practice the preparation we've been talking about; watching and working with role models will help you prepare for the role you are working toward.

Those are the truly successful people in any profession. They are the ones who have achieved great position and influence yet still have a strong family life and community life and live by a code of ethics and morality that earns them respect throughout their profession. Oftentimes you see successful people create bold initiatives to give back (i.e. Bono's (RED) campaign, the late Laura Ziskin's Stand Up to Cancer, the Bill & Melinda Gates Foundation). Once you've reached the top of the ladder, you realize that the top wasn't the only purpose; it was the climb that mattered as well. When you know you got help along the way, you naturally want to pay it forward. Giving, gratitude, compassion—those are the things that give the climb to the top of the career mountain its meaning.

So, start looking for those people who are steeped in humility, gratefulness, honesty, and consistency. Those are your role models for how to master your own Walk of Fame. They could be people in the corner offices at your company or the superstars in the worlds of entertainment, software, publishing, education, ministry, or sports. They might be your minister, a teacher, or even a member of your own family. Watch them. Listen to their stories. Pay close attention to how their words and actions align. Emulate them when appropriate. We all need people to lead us through the wilderness of success and its many temptations. Whether you are in Hollywood, finance, business, education, or any other field, it's easy to get lost in ego and self-praise. Identifying your role models can help you find yourself.

Who are my role models? My mother, my aunt Donna, my uncle, Pastor D. J. Williams, Muhammad Ali, Will Smith, Oprah, Joel Osteen, The Rock, my former bosses Elizabeth Cantillon and Ange Giannetti, Amy Pascal, and Stacey Snider. These are a few of the people—some of whom I know, some of whom I've only observed from afar—who have helped me manage my walk and to walk with purpose and peace.

HOW TO GET IN A "PRAISE MENTALITY"

The most genuinely successful people I know are also the most generous. They are the most giving of themselves, their time, and their money. They are the most generous with information and feedback. Many of them acknowledge God. The others who may not acknowledge God still acknowledge that they are blessed. For example, musician Chance the Rapper made headlines when he donated $1 million to Chicago's public school system, benefiting ten public elementary schools and high schools. This is one of the most generous donations to come out of the hip-hop community.

Generosity is a great place to start building your "praise mentality." Creating a mindset of praise will help you achieve your goals and dreams. Try the following:

- **Give of yourself.** The more you give, the more it will be given unto you. The Bible says it is better to give than to receive. That's why giving and helping others feels so good. When in doubt, give. When you're feeling low, help someone. When you're stuck, reach out and make a difference in someone else's life.

- **Deflect praise from yourself.** You've probably seen the speeches that the winners give at the Oscars or Golden Globe awards where they thank their agents, their directors, their mothers, and basically everyone else they've ever met. There's a reason for that, and it isn't just so that they appear humble. It's because the best in any profession understand that they did not achieve success alone. They also know that sharing praise with others and deflecting it from yourself is a sure way to remain motivated and hungry. Giving praise to others reminds you that you had help, from God to your colleagues to your mentors and even your friends. If you want to remain grounded, make sure you are the last person who gets credit for the great things you do. Make sure God is the first.

- **Build a praise team.** Sometimes, especially in highly competitive businesses such as entertainment, we treat success as a zero-sum game. In other words, for us to win, other people must lose. But that isn't how any industry really works. I've learned that peers support each other as we climb together; frequently, that's the only way the hard climb is bearable. So, ask yourself, have you been criticizing your rivals or supporting them as friends? It's nice to be happy for someone else's success, but it's even better to champion them.

  In fact, I would argue that true success is being in a position not only to wish someone else well but to help them advance in their own career without worrying about how their advancement will affect your career. Only someone working as hard as you are in the same profession can understand the workload and daily grind that you experience. So, celebrate your peers and colleagues, support them, and help them.

THOU SHALT

- » Take on a praise mentality, where you first praise God, then others.
- » Support, celebrate, and defend your peers, and expect them to do the same for you.
- » Avoid reading your own reviews.
- » Be the last one to celebrate and the first one back at work the next morning.

THOU SHALT NOT

- » Forget to pray after great successes and failures.
- » Sacrifice your lifestyle for your career and fall into the trap of "someday."
- » Overlook the people who shaped your character when you thank those who've helped you be successful.

8

YOUR DIFFERENCE IS YOUR DESTINY

> Not your thinking, but your being, is distinctiveness.
> Therefore not after difference, ye think it, must ye strive;
> but after your own being. At bottom, therefore, there is only
> one striving, namely, the striving after your own being.
> —Carl Jung

Hollywood respects the maverick, the person who's bold and daring, who's unique and has the confidence to defy the system and everyone who tells them they're wrong in order to follow their vision. One great example is a woman whom I'm blessed enough to know, one who has inspired me in every possible way. We all know her as Oprah, one of the most powerful figures in the world. But way back when, she was Oprah Winfrey, a news anchor in Baltimore who lost her job because she couldn't distance herself emotionally from the stories she covered. That's right—Oprah was demoted for being too emotional, told she was not right for television. That is until she was hired as the host of a Chicago morning talk show, where she wore her warm, emotional style on her sleeve. Audiences loved it, and the show, *The Oprah Winfrey Show*, became the highest-rated daytime program, ran for twenty-five years, and started a media empire. All because Oprah refused to change what made her different.

Again and again, we find that success comes from being the distinctive person that God created us to be. It's our differences, our uniqueness, that gets us to where we're supposed to be in life—our God-given destiny. It's not about trying to transform yourself into a vision of who other people want you to be or who your employer wants you to be. Understand what's required for your job but do it in a way that is authentically you. The quality that makes you unique—your talent, your style, your gift—is the very thing God will use to take you where you're supposed to be.

This isn't always easy, as Oprah found. People don't like what's different, and sometimes they criticize or ridicule people who insist on being different. It can be lonely. But even in the loneliness, you have to trust God and let your distinctiveness stand out. The moment you begin to exchange what makes you different for what makes you ordinary because you want to fit in, you give away that which God wants to use to elevate you and take you somewhere extraordinary.

In the church, there is a tendency to hammer down any nails that stick up. Churches often, intentionally or unintentionally, reinforce conformity. We're taught to blend in, assimilate, and be part of the congregation. Many times, thinking differently from the congregation or dressing differently is met with tremendous opposition. Very rarely does anyone in the church say, "At the end of the day, the thing that God created you to be, the uniqueness of you, needs to be embraced and cultivated." The church too often doesn't encourage us to ask critical, life-changing questions:

- "What makes me different?"

- "What makes me unique?"

- "What gives me a different worldview?"

- "Why do I think differently?"

- "How do I begin to embrace what makes me different and incubate it, instead of thinking 'I wish I were like everyone else'?"

Wishing to be like everyone else and wanting badly to fit in is understandable. It's tempting to try and mold your life so that someone else will approve of it. But that is a recipe for a fraudulent life of no peace, a life in which you will never achieve your destiny. Your distinction is who you are; it's the flavor God added to you that makes you like no one else. Salt is salt because when you put it on things, it lends a distinctive flavor. Distinctiveness makes people uneasy and it provokes, but it also intrigues and inspires. The greatest artists, inventors, and scientists are great because they embraced the differences God gave them. They took the tension between themselves and the mundane world around them and turned it into energy that powered their greatness. This can be your recipe for success.

SEQUEL-ITIS

The ironic thing about Hollywood is that while it's driven by truly daring, distinctive thinkers—the rebels and visionaries—who make films and TV shows like *Hidden Figures* or *Breaking Bad,* Hollywood is mostly a business that copies itself. The most valuable property in the industry isn't a new idea but a sequel or the next installment in a franchise, whether it's the next film to be released from the Marvel Cinematic Universe or a reboot of a reboot.

The great irony is that almost every time Hollywood plays it safe instead of embracing a new, bold, and possibly untested idea, failures ensue. Take these movies, for instance: *Alice Through the Looking Glass* (the sequel to *Alice in Wonderland*); *Bad Santa 2*; *Ben-Hur*; the *Ghostbusters* reboot; *Teenage Mutant Ninja Turtles: Out of the Shadows*; *The Huntsman: Winter's War*; *Zoolander No. 2*. All of these films were sequels or reboots that failed at the box office. When Hollywood copies what's been done or creates lifeless sequels as shortcuts to profitability, the results aren't pretty. All of those things are the opposite of being distinctive. You know that, when you see truly stunning, original work like *La La Land, Lion, Fences,* or *Beasts of the Southern Wild,* the brilliance of the work is only exceeded by the difficulty the filmmaker had in getting it made at all.

Deep down, we all know that taking risks and being different produces greatness. But we're terrified of it. We're herd animals, and we fear standing out. That's why public speaking is a greater fear than death for so many people. And if someone does manage to fight past that natural fear to try something original, they usually meet a wall of rejection: "No, you can't do that. That won't work."

Why? Dead silence. Remember what I said earlier? Most people don't really believe something is possible until someone does it. For rebels from Pablo Picasso to Albert Einstein to Francis Ford Coppola, that's been the case. It will be the case for you, too, and you have to fight it. But take heart in this chapter's Commandment:

Your Difference Is Your Destiny

You may have been advised to blend in and be like everyone else. That is the safer road, but it's not the one that leads to success. Remember that back in Chapter Two, I reminded you that God made you talent—endowed you with unique gifts and abilities as well as the desire to use them for His glory. Other people will not always understand those gifts; some will fear gifts that make you stand out in ways that make them uneasy. I'm here to tell you that the things that set you apart, the uniqueness that God gave you, the original ideas or idiosyncratic point of view you bring to your work—those are advantages to play up in your pursuit of your professional destiny, not weaknesses to hide.

I'm also aware that the qualities that make you different may make you uncomfortable as well because most of us fear being criticized. When you stand out, you face a greater risk of being noticed and critiqued or asked that awful question, "Do you think you're better than us?" But understand that God made you who you are for a *reason*. Whether you're different because of your appearance, your talents, the way your mind works, your political views, or anything else, God imbued you with those differences not so you would hide them but so you would use them and be proud of them. So, let's take a closer look at why you should be celebrating your differences, not hiding them.

False Idols

Difference for difference's sake is called being a *poseur,* and it won't win you any allies. If you have multiple body piercings or facial tattoos just for shock value, if you say outrageous things just to make people gasp—that doesn't make you original or a provocateur. It makes you a manipulator. The differences that matter are the authentic ones that reflect who you really are, and that includes distinctive qualities that you'd rather not share with anyone or that are subtle and hard to notice. Bottom line, to quote from Hamlet, "to thine own self be true." Don't try to be outrageous, humdrum, or anything in between. Be yourself as you really are. God made you that way, remember?

DESTINY IS A PROCESS

Destiny means that there is an area in which you're supposed to operate in order to produce the best results for yourself and God. It's your
highest purpose, your calling, your vocation. Reaching your destiny
always means passing through a process. If you respect and cultivate
the process, you will be successful and arrive where you're supposed
to arrive. Often, that means taking a winding, indirect, and unpre-
dictable path and trying things you don't expect: training for a new
position, stepping into a leadership role before you feel ready, putting
forth a daring idea that nobody else is ready to hear but you're confident in, or packing up everything you own to relocate and chase a
dream.

We live in a results-obsessed culture that can skew our idea of success. Thanks to technology, we can summon a ride or order a package
and have it nearly instantly, so we kid ourselves into believing that
results in our career should come as easily. I call it "smartphone success," because we act like success is as accessible as launching an app.
But if you dig into any field, you'll find that the true overnight success is as real as unicorns. No one—and I mean no one—reaches the
upper levels of their profession and enjoys the financial, lifestyle, and
status rewards that come at those levels in a short time. The overnight
sensation you heard about last week, whether it was a band, an author,
or a software entrepreneur, has put in at least ten years of work out of
the limelight in order to enjoy that "overnight" adulation.

If you want to start manifesting the destiny that God has set forth
for you, it's time to stop worrying so much about immediate results
and start appreciating the process that you're going through right at
this very moment. The process itself is a reward, not only because it
changes you but because your results will be far better when you ad-

here to it. When we try to circumvent the process or artificially speed it up, we damage our results. We don't allow our work and ourselves to evolve and grow.

From antique furniture to gourmet cheeses, there are many things that simply won't become what we want them to be without going through a time-consuming process to harness the distinctiveness that lies within. That beautiful golden patina that appears on some antiques is the result of chemical changes in the finish that can take decades. You can't fake that. The complex, exquisite flavor of some cheeses comes from aging, sometimes in deep caves or cellars, and the effects of mold, enzymes, and time. Maybe you could mimic the elements with chemistry, but you can't mimic the process, so the final result will never taste the same. *Your process is your result.*

How does this tie into our idea of difference and distinctiveness? Simple: no two persons' processes will ever be the same. The distinctiveness of your process and your experience shapes the result, makes it what it is. But beware of expecting your process to be predictable or even comfortable. You might think you're going to attend an Ivy League university, get your law degree, get a job at a white-shoe firm, and live happily ever after on Martha's Vineyard. But there will be detours along the way and turns you don't expect. There's a good reason for that:

We often mistake our purpose for God's.

You might have a career path in mind and a clear idea of how you will proceed from training and apprenticeship to upper management. That's great, but be wary not to follow a path that's your own without ensuring that it's God's path for you, too. The reality is that God may have a very different destiny in mind for you, and the process of realizing it might not look like what you think it should look like. But that doesn't mean it's the wrong process. So first, pray. Talk to the Lord and ask for clarity about the destiny He has set down for you. Then believe in the process and trust it. Even if it takes you places that are far different from what you had in mind, that's all right. Discomfort is often a sign that you're on the right path. To put it another way, just because your process is predictable and safe and you feel comfortable with it, that doesn't mean it's going to get you the results you want.

As I mentioned in *Produced by Faith*, I never wanted to be a studio executive. Early in my career, once I got an understanding of how the business worked, I said I would never work for a studio because I didn't want the studio executive lifestyle: the reading, the meetings, being on the go all the time. Yet, I made a commitment to follow the process for success wherever God led me. When the process took me to the gates of Metro-Goldwyn-Mayer, I had a choice: embrace the process and accept the studio executive job MGM was offering, or insist on having my own way and risk losing everything. I chose to take the job and that job unlocked the very thing I came to Hollywood for: to become a producer. Bottom line: trust God.

DON'T FEAR DISCOVERY, SEEK CONFIRMATION

Part of being distinctive is discovering yourself, and you can't be afraid of the process of discovery: seeing what you're good at, trying a few different things out, and not being afraid to fail. That's why it's important to avoid conventional wisdom and not listen to everyone's counsel, because you may need to try different jobs or skills that may seem ill-fitted on the surface. People who don't understand the value of your process will warn you away from the untrodden path when that's the path you need to be on!

In my process, the church did half the job and Hollywood did the other half. The church helped me learn how to be a leader and to take responsibility. Being an usher and a deacon and taking up the offering, helping the other deacons close up the church, helping prepare meals, and going out to feed the homeless—all of those things helped prepare me for responsibility, accountability, and leadership. I gained the opportunity to speak for the first time and develop that gift in the church. It was the incubator for my conventional side.

Hollywood gave me the opportunity to explore my unconventional side. Because I trusted God, I wasn't afraid to throw myself into a foreign environment where I had no friends at all. I wasn't afraid to say, "I believe I'm supposed to be here. Now let me put myself through a process to figure out what to do." Part of discovery is putting yourself in an environment that's scary but that moves you one step further along to where you're supposed to be.

A while ago, I posted a clip on Instagram in which I asked, "How can you be comfortable knowing that you are not living the fullness of your existence?" Meaning, be sure that you're not comfortable only because you've been *conditioned* to be. We can become conditioned to settle for less than we're capable of and tell ourselves we're happy. We can become conditioned to believe that God has nothing to say to us about our careers. We can become conditioned to believe what we see so that unless a career opportunity hits us across the head, we assume it's out of our reach. We can become conditioned to think the passion that keeps us up at night, that secret dream that we have, isn't real, but then we drag ourselves to a job that we convince ourselves *is* real. That conditioning keeps us from our destiny.

Being distinctive means fighting that cultural conditioning to conform, putting yourself into a process and discovering where you're supposed to be. There's nothing easy or safe about it. There's nothing predictable or comfortable about it. You try things that stretch you. You figure out what you can do in a way that no one else can. You figure out what makes you the handful of pepper in a pot of salt— what makes you unique. And you run with that, letting no one tell you otherwise. Once you're in an environment and you're doing what you believe you're destined to do, notice the type of feedback that you get. What's the response when you use your gift? Are people validating it? Are they receiving it? Are other professionals in the same field acknowledging you as a peer?

When I was an executive, feedback from my superiors let me know I was on the right path:

- "Wow, DeVon. The way you handled yourself in that meeting was great."

- "Your thoughts on that script are terrific."

- "You got a song from Alicia Keys for our movie? That's amazing."

Throughout my process in entertainment, while I was learning and discovering how to use my gifts, I got confirmation of my gifting that let me know to keep going. Look for signs that God is sending you confirmation. Going back to Daniel and Shadrach and Meshach and Abednego in Babylon, they got confirmation that they were heading in the right direction.

Daniel's gift to interpret dreams was confirmation that he was on the path to be a leader. When he explained Nebuchadnezzar's dream and articulated what was going to happen, and then it actually happened, that was confirmation. When they all went through the fire and did not get burned, that was confirmation. When Daniel went into the lion's den and did not get eaten, that was confirmation. God will send you signs: people, opportunities, praise. When you receive them, acknowledge God's gift and then say, "Hey, I'm exactly where I'm supposed to be, and I'm doing exactly what I'm supposed to do." It's a great feeling.

However, to get confirmation you have to risk criticism. Being different, not conforming, daring to stand out—these can lead to criticism even if you're doing great work. But you can't let that stop you. We're so afraid of criticism that we become risk averse, so we avoid putting ourselves in situations where people might offer even constructive criticism. If you're afraid of being criticized, you may miss out on the moments of confirmation that give you the motivation and hope to keep moving.

Exodus

The organization you work for should celebrate your differences, not suppress them. If you prove that you're valuable and you want to carve out a space within a company or agency to do things your own way, you should be able to. I did it when I created my own little niche at Sony, but I was able to do so because I'd earned it. If you've done the time and proved that you're valuable, but you're not allowed to bring some of your own distinctive vision to your job, you're in the wrong place.

BE CAREFUL NOT TO BE CAREFUL

The other way people let their distinctiveness fade is by getting careful. For example, in 1982, Michael Jackson released *Thriller,* without a doubt one of the greatest albums ever made. Then, after a five-year wait, he released his follow-up, *Bad* . . . and the world kind of said, "Really?" I mean, the record had some big hits on it, but after the incredible orig- inality and artistry of *Thriller,* it was obvious that *Bad* was just more of the same with different packaging. After that record, Michael remained a huge star, but many critics said he had peaked as a recording artist.

That's a classic example of being careful when you should be bold, and it happens all the time. When we achieve some success, our dis- tinction suddenly gains notoriety and at the same time runs the risk of losing its uniqueness. When you're unknown, you can be as differ- ent, daring, and provocative as you want, because nobody is watching. Then success comes, and you can start to fear not being able to dupli- cate the success you just achieved. So, instead of taking risks and find- ing even more distinctiveness, you can just try to repeat what you've already done.

The irony of success is that when you try to be more than a "one- hit wonder," you can stop listening to your creative heart and the vi- sion given to you by God and start looking at only marketing data and trends . . . and thus *guarantee* that you will be a one-hit wonder. How often have you seen a novelist or musician come out of nowhere and take the world by storm with their first commercial release only to bomb with the second? They didn't suddenly stop being talented! They started worrying about being successful instead of being original.

You *will* be tempted to play it safe. That's probably what you're doing right now. But playing it safe isn't doing anyone any favors— especially yourself. If you aren't playing it safe, good for you, but be hyperaware of the natural tendency to keep playing the same note over and over. You may think you have your career wired at some point and that all you need to do is keep replicating what you did yes- terday to keep having rewarding tomorrows. But that's not the path to sustainable success. Sustainable success comes when you keep displaying the unique light that God gave you where everyone can see it.

How do you maintain your distinctiveness in the face of success? How do you keep from losing your edge? First, stop worrying about doing what other people will like. That's the path to ruin. Instead, as you become successful, continue to fill your heart, mind, body, and spirit with things that edify you emotionally and spiritually, so that you have a deeper well to draw from. You can get tapped out, you know. When you're fighting for your position and trying to make it to the top, sleeping on people's couches, interning, and working for free, you won't have trouble motivating your spirit and keeping that hunger burning. But once you start finding success and living in the calling of your life, it's harder to keep in touch with what sets your soul on fire. The greats find a way to stay on that edge, stay dissatisfied, stay provocative, and they do it by being true to what *they* want to see and read and hear, not what anyone else wants.

Pray. Meditate. Get out in nature. Travel. Read. Stay in church. Employ a wide variety of methods to stay in close touch with God's voice inside you that's always saying, "Not good enough. You can do more. Make them sweat. Take a chance." Remember how we talked about your gut? Trust your gut, that place where God's voice and nudging often hides. As your career advances, keep pushing the boundaries of your abilities and your profession. Don't lose the edge that got you where you are.

NO BORROWED DISTINCTIVENESS

Back in 2009, when I was in Beijing working on *The Karate Kid,* there was a moment that crystallized for me what's so challenging about holding on to our distinctive qualities in a world that really wants us to be like everybody else. We were just sitting on the set between shots and I was watching Will Smith and his family—Jada, Jaden, and Willow—hanging out and having fun and playing around. As I sat there enjoying them, God spoke to me in my spirit, saying, *What do you see?*

I said, *I see the Smith family.*

God wasn't settling for that. *What do you really see?*

I looked closer, and what I really saw was a family having fun. If not for them, there would be no *The Karate Kid*—it was their movie. They were making this film on their summer break and it was a family affair. As an executive, part of the way that you cope with the day-to-day stress is by making yourself believe that you're more important and integral to things than you really are. I was telling myself, "I'm an integral part of *The Karate Kid*. This movie wouldn't have happened without me."

God's revelation was, *Yeah, you're a part of it, but it still would have happened anyway. It's their movie, not yours.*

He kept making His point, loud and clear: *DeVon, if this movie comes out of their distinctiveness, it doesn't get credited to you. This movie wasn't birthed out of what makes you distinctive. You're servicing this movie for the Smith family. You're servicing their distinctiveness. Don't mistake someone else's distinctiveness for your own distinctiveness.*

I know, right? *Lord, that was brutal.*

But He was right. And at that moment, I determined that I would become everything God ordained me to be and that I would stop playing it safe. I knew I hadn't been created to service someone else's distinctiveness for the rest of my life. But if I was going to figure out what my real distinctiveness was, I had to make myself intensely uncomfortable. This thinking led to the revelations later on that trip to China that ended up as the foundation of *Produced by Faith*.

That was a revelatory, if difficult, conversation with God. If He hadn't made me face the cold reality that I was servicing someone else's distinctiveness, not my own, I can't say for sure that I would have ever really challenged myself to figure out what makes me distinctive and what God wanted me to say. I might have continued to borrow other people's distinctiveness. It can be tempting to do that, believe me. You work for a company that engineers bold, new products, manage a gallery for a groundbreaking artist, or date someone with a totally original sense of style, and you think that being in *proximity* to distinctiveness *makes you distinctive*. It doesn't. That's a lie we tell ourselves when we fear getting out there, expressing our differences and our talent, and risking ridicule or failure.

You cannot borrow distinction, and you don't need to. God gave you vision, talents, drive, a way of thinking—something—that makes you unique and unlocks your destiny. It can be a chore to find it, but you'll never find it if you're busy basking in the reflected glory of someone else's uniqueness. Instead, do your homework. Know what people are making, buying, and liking so you're not duplicating what's already out there. Discover where your voice fits and where the seams are. What can you say and do that will make your voice stand out in a crowded field? Most important, what is everyone else afraid to do? Find out and do it.

If it's hard (and it is), do it anyway. Being different is not a state of mind but a *habit*. Do you think those designers and artists and surfers and musicians who look and live in such provocative ways have always been like that? No. They made a choice at some point to be who they were and dare to stand out. The sky didn't fall, they liked it, and they kept doing it. Eventually, their difference became part of their brand. There is no reason you can't do the same thing. God wants you to embrace your difference and live boldly.

SPIRITUAL PRINCIPLES, SECULAR SUCCESS

However, not everyone else does. Until you are on top of your profession (and sometimes, even then) you will face pressure to conform, hide what makes you different, and be like everyone else. Some of the pressure will come from people jealous of what you've accomplished, while some will come from those who simply fear what's different. How do you resist the pressure to conform?

First of all, consider this text from Romans 12:1–2 (MSG):

So, here's what I want you to do, God helping you: Take your everyday, ordinary life—your sleeping, eating, going-to-work, and walking-around life—and place it before God as an offering. Embracing what God does for you is the best thing you can do for him. Don't become so well-adjusted to your culture that you fit into it without even thinking. Instead, fix your attention on God. You'll be changed from the inside out. Readily recognize what he wants from you, and quickly respond to it. Unlike the culture around you, always dragging you down to its level of immaturity, God brings the best out of you, develops well-formed maturity in you.

Don't worry about the culture around you. That's my first piece of advice. Pray and focus on what God wants of you because He'll be very clear about it if you let Him. Beyond that, all you can do is fight conformity like hell. Part of playing the game in your career is saying, "I understand what my organization needs me to do, and I'll do it to the best of my ability but not to the detriment of what makes me distinctive."

I was in an animation meeting, and a storyboard artist brought up a great analogy about this. He said, "When you go to the supermarket and walk into the cookie aisle, how many different brands of chocolate chip cookie are there? Probably thirty. Well, each one is the same kind of cookie, just with a different recipe."

Conformity says, "Be like that person." Distinctiveness says, "I know what I have to do professionally and I'll get it done, but I'm going to do it using my recipe, and I won't change my recipe into someone else's." You fight conformity by trusting and believing that the distinctiveness that God gave you is the key to your success. You use it and rely on it until you get success and validation, which keeps you going. You keep your edge, and you don't get lazy so that you don't become "sanded down"—a blander version of somebody else. Once you do that, it's hard to come back. If an employer or audience can get the real thing, why would they want you?

Away from the Workplace

Many of us have a creative side. We play an instrument, write fiction, or make furniture as hobbies, and maybe we even dream idly about doing those things for a living. But . . . and that's where the conversation stops. But why? Why not try just once to make a career out of a passion? To give yourself the best chance of success, focus on being different. Instead of writing a Harry Potter knockoff, write something crazily original. Instead of having your band sound like everyone else on the Top 40, come up with your own unique sound. Who cares if it's popular? Unique, challenging, and brave are more important. Besides, you have nothing to lose and everything to gain.

HOW TO CULTIVATE YOUR DISTINCTIVENESS

- **Hang with original thinkers.** Spend time with people from all walks of life who are challenging the status quo, producing original work, and refusing to conform. Be sure they're not people who simply look the part but are afraid of defying convention; those are easy to find. Instead, hang with those who appreciate your distinctive thinking but also challenge it.

- **Ask forgiveness, not permission.** Don't seek people's approval before you do something that expresses your uniqueness or originality; just do it. I'm not telling you to do something that violates the rules of your workplace and gets you disciplined, just not to look for anyone to validate what you want to try before the fact. Commonly, well-meaning individuals will try to talk you out of actions they feel are risky, not understanding that taking them is critical to your growth and advancement.

- **Go where the crowd isn't going.** When you've surveyed the landscape of your profession or industry and seen what the herd is doing in terms of creativity, business ideas, marketing, or anything else, pivot 180 degrees and go in the other direction. It's like the advice you'll often hear about the stock market: *when the crowd is selling, buy, and when the crowd is buying, sell.* People flock together for validation and safety; no one wants to be the one in the herd who stands out and gets taken down. But you're no herd animal. You're an original. Be the first one to go in your direction and make everyone else follow *you.*

- **Don't focus on keeping what you have.** Playing it safe is basically saying, "I don't trust my instincts, passion, faith, or God and I'm afraid if I don't repeat what I did last year, I'll lose my nice house and nice car." Train yourself not to worry about keeping anything. You're only renting it from God anyway. Don't attach to what you have and, strangely, you'll have more.

- **Create silence to listen to your inner voice.** Find times and places of peace that allow you to quiet your mind, talk to God, and listen to your nagging, tugging, motivating inner voice. That's where you'll hear the Lord speaking to you in ideas that you can't get out of your head, thrilling brainstorms that you stay up all night working on, and the courage to stand out from the crowd.

THOU SHALT

» Know what other people in your field are doing.
» Identify role models who are proudly distinctive.
» Eagerly embrace the process of becoming who you're destined to be.

THOU SHALT NOT

» Mistake distinctive packaging with distinctive impact on the world.
» Apologize for being different from others.
» Create to please others instead of yourself.

9

YOUR AMNESIA IS AN ASSET

> To be able to forget means sanity.
> —Jack London

The problem with taking the world by storm is that as soon as the applause stops, everyone says, "That was great. Can you do it again?" That's never truer than in Hollywood, where you're only as hot as your last project. That's why it's so important to have a short memory. The perfect example of this, to me, is M. Night Shyamalan. He blew everyone's minds with the movie *The Sixth Sense*, right? *Unbreakable* and *Signs* were huge box office hits as well. He was on the cover of *Newsweek* in August of 2002 under a headline that read, "The Next Spielberg." I mean, no pressure, right?

Then his career fell off a cliff. He couldn't buy a hit. Almost every one of his movies from 2006 to 2016 failed to achieve the heights of his early career successes. *Lady in the Water, The Happening, The Last Airbender, After Earth*—they all failed miserably. Even the ones that did okay at the box office were critical flops. It got to the point where he'd become a pop-culture joke. But in January 2017, he released *Split,* a movie he'd made for only $9 million, a fraction of what a movie like *After Earth* cost. That film has been a smash hit—well-reviewed, earning more than $40 million in its first weekend and more than $275 million worldwide as of this writing. As someone who knows how incredibly hard it is to make a good movie and to repeat successes, I'm thrilled for Shyamalan.

But what really impresses me about him isn't his films. It's his ability to erase his past failures and the avalanche of criticism from his mind and keep going—to keep believing in his talent and his vision. If he hadn't been able to do that, he would have been so consumed with his failures that he could have never harnessed the power and the talent within him to achieve the success that *Split* has been. Now, he's pretty much got his career back. In fact, after the 2017 Academy Awards fiasco, where Best Picture was mistakenly awarded to *La La Land* when *Moonlight* had actually won, Shyamalan, with wonderful self-deprecation, tweeted that he had written the twist ending. If you're going to survive in any field, you just can't take yourself too seriously. Having a short memory goes a long way.

THE VALUE OF FORGETTING

God has given us a vision of who we are and what we're supposed to be. Every day that we get closer to that, we're happier. Every day we move further from it, we feel it, consciously or subconsciously. When things happen that upset us or delay us, or when we experience frustrations and setbacks, the challenge we face is to hold on to that vision, keep trusting and feeding the talent that we know we have, and not let our failures make us doubt who we are.

As we've already discussed, when you try to do something big, the world pushes back. So, you need a mentality and a mindset that's rock-solid clear about who you are, what you're supposed to do, and where you're supposed to go. It's critical. In the church, we preach this idea that God forgives us and as long as we confess our sins, he forgives and he forgets. The problem is that while we may be forgiven, we never forget what we did wrong. We internalize those things, and those are the very things that begin to hinder our belief in ourselves.

Ego also trips us up because, at the end of the day, we're human. One of the reasons we love being successful isn't just because we draw closer to the future God has in mind for us, but because we love basking in the adulation. That's normal and there's nothing wrong with it . . . for a little while. The trouble comes when your ego becomes so insatiable that it won't tolerate failure or even the risk of failure. That's when some people stop taking chances and sometimes stop creating altogether. The terror of not being able to live up to past success becomes so overwhelming that it paralyzes them. That could have happened to Shyamalan. But the thing that I find so fascinating is that he clearly never stopped believing that he was still M. Night Shyamalan. Even though everyone in Hollywood said, "He's lost his fastball. He doesn't know how to direct anymore," and while he may have internalized some of that stuff, he obviously figured it out and kept going. He kept creating until he created something great.

You may have been taught in the church to remember the lessons of failure, pride, and even humiliation because by remembering them, we're more likely to be humble before God. But I want to suggest that there's even greater power in forgetting those things because it's only when we turn away from our past shortcomings that we can live for the future—where God has great things in mind for us. That's why I've identified this Commandment:

Your Amnesia Is an Asset

Amnesia allows you to keep going in the face of failure and criticism. Because you will fail. You will make bad judgment calls. You will be tempted to cling to the past. And you will definitely be criticized. But life is about moving forward, and sometimes forgetting is the best way to keep doing exactly that. Let's explore all the ways that forgetting is an asset.

ASK FORGIVENESS, NOT PERMISSION

I've found that the people who are the most successful tend to have the shortest memories. They draw a clear line between the external and the internal—

External: Trends, tastes, luck, criticism from others
Internal: Vision, belief, self-criticism, faith

—and they don't confuse the two. They understand that the external is beyond their control, so while it might wash against them like the tide against rocks, they don't let it break them down. They know that no matter what they do, no matter how good their work or honest their effort, some failures are out of our control—as are some successes. They might listen to the criticism, but they also know when listening becomes counterproductive. At some point, they're able to turn away, ignore the waves that keep beating against the rocks, and get back to work.

The internal is where we can sabotage ourselves. We hold on to regrets, recriminations, and self-accusations too long. I have seen talented individuals in entertainment hang on to disappointments, frustrations, ugly comments, and projects that didn't quite work out for so long that negativity infected them like a virus of self-doubt, ultimately preventing them from ever doing the kind of work they could have done. That's not just the case for a creative profession like filmmaking, writing, or art, either; it's true for anyone who dares to stick their necks out to try and do something ambitious, from a company project to a business startup. When you stick your neck out, no matter how prepared or talented you are, *somebody* will swing a sword at it—or worse, ignore it.

Another quality shared by the most successful people in any industry is the ability to get up and keep going time after time like they never fell down at all. One great example is Amazon CEO Jeff Bezos. He put huge resources and personal vision behind the Amazon Fire Phone—his attempt to compete with Apple's iPhone. The Fire Phone was a flop that cost millions . . . but Bezos didn't hesitate. He took the energy and vision behind that product, pivoted, and led his engineering team to come up with the voice-controlled Echo home assistant (the "Alexa, play my music" device), which has not only become a massive hit but is changing how people interact with their homes—and even how they speak.

That fast pivot, not looking back or dwelling on failure, turns boldness into greatness. Sometimes, what other people call genius is not a matter of being smarter or more talented than everyone else but simply being stubborn and persistent enough to keep putting ideas into the world until one of them catches fire. You don't ask for permission or approval from anyone. In the last chapter, I said that it is better to apologize than ask permission. The idea is that being assertive and taking the initiative is preferable to worrying about what people are saying. If you hit a wall on a project or an idea, and you ask someone else for their advice before getting back on the horse, they might try to stop you from getting back on at all. Worse, you might listen.

Successful people keep pushing because they know if they stop, they could lose their momentum. Doubt can seep into even the most confident heart. If you find reasons to hesitate, your work might come to a dead stop. In any profession, momentum is everything. You should always be working on the next big idea, the next invention, the next acquisition—the next *something*. If you get your hand slapped because you acted too aggressively, so what?

I have a simple process you can follow when you're considering an action that might be too aggressive. To decide if you should ask permission or just go ahead, answer:

- Is what I'm planning to do likely to get me fired?

- Does it go against my publicly stated values and my private knowledge of what I stand for?

- Does it go against the destiny God has set down for me?

If the answer to even one of the questions is "Yes" or even "Maybe," stop and seek counsel. Otherwise, proceed with confidence. This does not mean you won't encounter resistance, criticism, and even anger from others, especially if what you do defies what they expect of you. Even if your choice is wildly successful, you will always find people who resent that you did something other than what they expected of you. As we said when we talked about talent, many people are most comfortable when they can put those around them into boxes. This lets them know exactly what to expect from everybody else and prevents uncomfortable surprises. But here's a truth:

Someone else's discomfort with your
bold action is not your problem.

Back in Chapter Five, I implored you to trust your gut instinct because that is God speaking to you at a level beyond reason and rationality. Well, when you're facing a choice between bold action you know to be right and risking the disapproval of others because of that choice . . . you know which one to choose. You can't please others at the expense of doing what you know to be right. You have two primary duties in this world: be a person of honor, character, and morality, and be true to the purpose God has placed in your heart. If you are doing both, it really doesn't matter what anyone else thinks of your career choices.

False Idols

It's one thing to keep pushing when you know you have a unique vision that demands expression. It's another to keep making the same mistakes over and over because you're too stubborn to change your strategy. What sets the greats apart from the also-rans is not only that they didn't give up but that they continually tried new things, figuring that one day, one of their new ideas would be a breakthrough. Persistence is a virtue, but mindless repetition is not.

FORGETTING YOUR SUCCESSES

In this chapter, I'm going to talk about some of the many things that are worth forgetting. The first is your successes. If it's important to forget about your failures and the self-doubt they breed, it's just as essential to forget about your successes and the overconfidence they create. A wise man once said, "Winning makes you lazy and stupid," and I couldn't agree more. When you have a great success, the lesson you can take away from it is that you're entitled to it because you're just smarter and more talented than everyone else. But if that's what you remember from your victories, you're more likely to coast on what you think makes you more deserving than others. Even if you do that subconsciously, you can lose your edge and make repeating your success impossible.

If you want to avoid the dreaded "sophomore slump," the best thing you can do is unlearn everything you learned about being a winner. Think back to *Star Wars: The Empire Strikes Back* (for my money, the best film in the franchise). There's a classic section in that movie where Luke Skywalker has gone to the planet Dagobah to find Yoda, the Jedi Grand Master, so Yoda can teach him how to use the Force. When Luke finally locates the tiny master, Yoda finds it necessary to deprogram Luke from his understanding of the natural world and reorient him with how things really work—with the unseen Force that guides the universe. In one scene, he even tells Luke, "You must unlearn what you have learned." If Luke can let go of past failures and trust the Force, he will be able to harness a power that few in the cosmos can use.

I'm not a killjoy. It's okay to enjoy a success. It's okay to take a victory lap. Believe me, I savored the calls I got after *Heaven Is for Real* and *Miracles from Heaven;* I enjoyed basking in the results of all that hard work—for a day. Then I got back to work. I didn't let it go to my head because I remembered two things. First, believing in your own greatness is a sure way to kill it. Ego makes you lazy and makes you take shortcuts, which spell doom for any ambitious goal. Second, I keep in mind that everything I achieve is due to God working through me, and it's all for His glory. That keeps me humble because I know that if I fall into the trap of believing my own press clippings, I might lose sight of who I am.

So yes, enjoy the victory lap. Just make it a short one. Savor it, give thanks, then get up the next morning and get back to work.

Exodus

There is one instance in which you should ignore my advice to forget your failures and keep going. If what you're doing is changing who you are on a fundamental level and pulling you away from God and the person He created you to be, take your failure as a message. Because there are many ways to fail, and the worst has nothing to do with losing money or opportunity. It has to do with losing *yourself.* If you feel like a failure occurred not because of bad luck or bad timing but because the pressure to succeed is making you into someone you don't want to be, get out. No success is worth distancing yourself from the Lord.

FORGETTING PAST GLORY

My grandfather was a wonderful man, but he tended to live in the rosy past instead of the present. He was a great baseball player in high school (he could play a mean game of basketball, too), and he probably had the talent to play baseball professionally. But he didn't, and while he had a full life, he always felt like his best years were in the rearview mirror. His favorite topic of conversation was his athletic glory days, just like in the Bruce Springsteen song.

Memories of past glories are fun, but what happens when you hold on to a memory for too long? You start living in the past and losing enthusiasm for the present. The present is dull, cast in uncertainties and shades of gray; in the past, you were the winning quarterback or the prom queen. When you live in the past, you're living as the person you were, and that's not who God wants you to be. He wants you to be who you are today and to become who you're destined to become.

You won't do that if your first words are always, "Remember when . . ."

Never forget the glory days, but don't relive them. Don't dwell in or on them. Let them be what they are: a shining moment that propels you forward.

FORGETTING PAIN

Another important thing to forget is past pain and guilt. But boy, do we love to hold on to both! I have known people who were so consumed by pain from their past or by guilt from some sin that had been forgotten by everyone else, that they simply could not move forward in life. In those situations, pain and guilt become excuses for not trying. "I failed because of that trauma from my childhood" or "I can't do that because I'll just let everyone down like before" are the kinds of things you hear from people who cannot forget pain and guilt. The thing is, while there is value in remembering things like past glories, there is no value in holding on to emotional pain and guilt. They are useless emotions that we cling to in order to punish ourselves.

That's why we have to engage in the act that is at the center of Christianity: *forgiveness*. God forgives all if we come to him asking forgiveness, but sometimes we forget to forgive ourselves. Forgetting pain and guilt means forgiving yourself for whatever is making you hold on to either one. Even Paul the Apostle had to have amnesia about his former life as a Christian prosecutor. If he had wallowed in the guilt of his past, he never would have gone on to write most of the New Testament that helped shape modern Christianity.

Paul was able to move beyond his story and not be held back, because he forgot about his pain and guilt. He didn't forget the lessons of those experiences, but he stopped letting them determine what he could do and who he could be.

HOLLYWOOD AMNESIA AND PERSONAL HUMILIATION

Even Hollywood, for all its reputation for venality and egotism, is a surprisingly amnesiac place, even for people who have humiliated or damaged themselves beyond what seems like all hope of redemption. Look at the careers of Robert Downey Jr. and Mel Gibson. Once, they were huge talents, superstars with the world at their feet. Then, they fell prey to fame. Downey lost himself in drug abuse and was widely seen as a lost cause, impossible to work with. Then, director Jon Favreau was making a "little" superhero movie in 2007 and wanted to cast Downey in the starring role. The producers were uneasy, but Downey cleaned himself up, behaved like a total pro, and turned *Iron Man* into a blockbuster and the foundation of a franchise. All was forgotten once Downey's work ethic and professionalism caught up with his talent.

As for Gibson, who should've been riding high for life after successes like the Oscar-winning *Braveheart,* he did his best to destroy his career not once but twice. First, in 2006, he was pulled over for driving under the influence and exploded into an anti-Semitic tirade. Second, in 2010 he left horrifying phone messages for Oksana Grigorieva, with whom he had a daughter, and was later found to be under a restraining order for domestic abuse. William Morris, his representatives, dropped him, and Hollywood blackballed him for the better part of a decade.

In one of the great ironies of this business, in 2014 one of the voices urging Hollywood to forgive Gibson for his transgression was Robert Downey Jr. Then, in 2016, Gibson made the film *Hacksaw Ridge,* which earned six Oscar nominations, winning two. Suddenly, all was forgotten. Creative Artists Agency (CAA) picked him up as a client, and now he's in line to direct the next installment in the blockbuster *Suicide Squad* franchise.

Sometimes it takes a while to get back, but you can't allow the memory of a bad choice or humiliating reversal to hold you back. Most people and most industries are very forgiving. God is forgiving. Forgive yourself, forget, and move forward.

WHAT NOT TO FORGET

There's something so vital here that I can't believe I almost forgot to talk about it. Here it is:

Forgetting doesn't mean forgetting everything.

Forgetting isn't pretending that something didn't happen. It's not forgetting the lessons you learned during those hard times or poor choices. It's not forgetting the joy of your glory days or the people who made them possible. I'm not talking about forgetting your car keys or phone. Forgetting means a lot of things in a Commandments context:

1. **To stop reliving the past to the degree that it negatively impacts your present and future.** What memories of the past are you reliving that you need to let go of today? Why are you reliving them? Here's a simple test: if the memories make you feel good, then store them away like photos in an album. If they make you feel pain, then let them go. Stop dwelling in them.

2. **To stop letting your past pass judgment on your present.** What happened in the past might have been a judgment on who you were then, but that was then. You're not the same person. You've

grown and moved closer to the full realization of God's destiny for you. And if God finds you worthy, you're worthy.

3. **To stop letting the past define what you can do.** My skill set isn't the same as it was ten years ago; neither is yours. My judgment is better than it was ten years ago; so is yours. You are not the same person you were in the past, and failure doesn't mean you lack the talent to achieve your purpose. The greats all failed. But they did not allow that failure to define them.

4. **To stop thinking you know more than God.** That's what the stubborn refusal to forget really is: the assertion that you, not God, decide your worth. Well, God has already declared your worth and found you equal to His purpose, so why are you fighting so hard against His judgment? Accept that God has already forgiven and forgotten, and so can you.

Of course, there are things you should remember from your past successes, failures, glories, and pain. Amnesia is about turning your back on self-doubts, slights from others, and the nagging fear that you don't have what it takes. Anything that feels like a judgment that could stop you from moving on to the next thing, you should cast it from you and leave it behind. But make sure you don't forget the lessons and skills you've learned along the way.

When M. Night Shyamalan endured all those box office and critical flops, he might have found a way to forget about the critiques and the jokes and the embarrassment, but he obviously didn't forget how to be a filmmaker. He learned from each project about how to compose a shot, how to write a stronger screenplay, how to use subtle changes in lighting—the million subtle skills that make a filmmaker an artist. He didn't throw that baby out with the critical bathwater. So, confronting failure becomes as much about what you keep and remember as what you forget and discard as irrelevant.

Self-defeating beliefs? Discard. Professional relationships? Keep. Trolling from people who don't know anything about your profession? Discard. Processes and systems that make you more efficient and productive? Keep. See what I'm getting at? Keep what helps you become better and smarter and more skilled over time; dump what threatens to sabotage what you believe you can achieve. This becomes a virtuous cycle, because the more you keep going back to the well and trying again and again, the more you'll learn and the better you'll get at whatever it is you do. *Persistence becomes proficiency* . . . IF you are doing what God has meant for you to do.

That's where the church can play an important role. If you want to be certain that you're still on the career path that God has in mind for you, check in with your pastor or church elder from time to time and talk about it. Are you praying in a way that leaves you open to the Word and doesn't just validate what you want to believe? Are you correctly interpreting the signs that God is placing in your path? You might absolutely be on the right career track, but it's still reassuring to check back in with the church and get confirmation that what you believe you're hearing and feeling when you engage with the Lord is right.

If it helps, make a list of what not to forget as you move from venture to venture, project to project, and job to job: skills, life lessons, pieces of wisdom, specific knowledge, people, and anything else that you think can carry over from what you just did to what you might do tomorrow and make you better.

Away from the Workplace

I'm not a parent, but I know many people who are wonderful parents, and they give me the same piece of advice for the day when I do become a parent: go easy on yourself. Raising another human being is hard, important work, and there will be times when you fall short of the parent you want to be. You'll raise your voice, lose your temper, or say something you shouldn't. Then, you'll crush yourself with guilt over it. Don't. We all fall, and parents are no different. As my friends with kids remind me, what matters is that you heal the breach, get back to love and protection and respect, and learn from your mistake. God can be a harsh parent, but He loves us unconditionally. Whatever mistakes you make, your love for your kids transcends them. Learn and let the rest go.

REMEMBER WHO YOU ARE

Samson was one of the strongest people mentioned in the Bible, and the key to his supernatural strength was his hair. We all know what happened with Samson: after multiple attempts, Delilah was finally successful in getting him to reveal the secret to his strength, and when the Philistines cut it off, his power left him, and they gouged out his eyes and forced him to grind grain in prison. However, one day Samson remembered who he was and who God was and asked God to return his power so he could complete his mission. God answered his prayer, and Samson succeeded in destroying the Philistines even though it cost him his life in the process.

I mentioned that maintaining who you are—who God wants you to be—throughout your career is what keeps you on the path to having the career of your dreams. Well, that might be the most important lesson of this chapter. As vital as it is to have amnesia when it comes to failures and doubt, you have to remember who you are and the talent you have. Like Samson at the end of the story, you set everything else aside, put your head down, and keep believing. You say what I say to myself:

> **"I keep going. I keep progressing. I keep pushing.**
> **I keep affirming who I am. I keep creating. I keep writing.**
> **I keep directing. I keep teaching. I keep going, and I don't**
> **let anything that's happened in my past affect my future."**

The past is the past. The more you stay in the past, the harder it is to live in the future. You cannot let anything you go through make you forget who you are or your belief that you are capable of whatever God has told you that you are capable of. If you lose that faith, you're really losing faith in God. If you lose faith in who you were created to be, you're doubting Him. Who has a say in how your career and life progress? Some supervisor? Some online commenter? Or the One who made you to be who you are?

The Karate Kid gave me my first powerful lesson in the necessity of self-belief. That was a super-successful picture that made $90 million in profit for Sony. It had a $56 million opening weekend and was so successful that on Monday, the chairperson threw an impromptu party for our entire division to congratulate everybody. The only other film she ever did that for during my time at Sony was *Spider-Man*. I had been the studio executive on that film and shepherded it from development all the way to production, and it was so successful that I thought I might get bumped up the ladder from junior executive to senior executive.

But not long after the film's debut, my boss had me in for a meeting and said, "DeVon, *The Karate Kid* was great. What you did was amazing. But we have so many senior executives that you're going to have to get used to still being a junior executive for a while." I was more than frustrated; I was mad. Normally, if you work on a big movie like that, it propels your career forward. It helps you get promoted. It helps you build a business. I said, "Wait a minute. Why is this working differently for me?" I'd just had a huge success, and they were telling me that I had to "get used to" being a junior executive? I felt slighted and overlooked.

Two things helped me get past that time and move forward. The first was setting my ego aside. I remembered that everything I had and did was about God's glory, not mine. Second, I remembered who He had told me I was. To myself, I said, "I don't accept what you're trying to put on me. I understand that there may be certain parts of my job that I don't like that I'm going to have to do, but I will not take on the identity of a junior executive. I am more than that. I will not take on the identity of someone who's incapable of running a movie or putting a movie together. I know who I am. I know the talent that I have, and I'm going to find a way to build on that even if you aren't going to give me the opportunity." And then I went back to work.

What came out of that was *Jumping the Broom*. I found a way to get that movie done (and of course, really got to know the marvelous lady who became my wife). What came out of that was *Heaven Is for Real*. All those things came out of my own initiative and desire and belief in who I was and my conviction about what I could do. By doing those movies outside of my main division at Sony, I took the risk that the people that I worked with would be mad at me and things might not work out well. But the risk that one of those movies wouldn't work was something I had to accept because making those films was *who I was*. I kept my belief in my talent, in my gift. I went back to work the next day, sat down at my desk, took a deep breath, and got back to it.

If we pursue who we are without apology, we will get up in the morning and become whoever God wants us to be. I try to do that daily. So should you. If you have what it takes and you believe it, ignore what people say, and do the job. People's doubts are not your problem. Just because they cast doubt in your direction doesn't mean you have to catch it. It has nothing to do with your belief in who you are. That's between you and God.

Sometimes, the greatest magic is the power to turn the page. I had setbacks. You'll have them. They're temporary. God isn't. Learn to know the difference and amnesia will become your ally.

THOU SHALT

» Have your next moves mapped out in advance.
» Stay humble in the face of success.
» Have spiritual counselors to help you bounce back from a loss.

THOU SHALT NOT

» Get overconfident.
» Listen to trolls.
» Neglect the skills that make you a pro.

10

YOUR WORLD IS SMALLER THAN YOU THINK

If you want to go fast, go alone. If you want to go far, go with others.
—African proverb

There's an app I use called Living Earth. It lets you know the weather in any part of the world as well as the sunrise and sunset times. One of the coolest features is the locator button: you can hit it and get a live picture of the rotating Earth with a small, glowing blue dot showing you where you are. When I see that dot in reference to the rest of world, it's an overwhelming feeling that reminds me of how vast the world really is. Many times, when we're reminded that we're just a little blue dot on a planet of more than 7.3 billion people, it's easy to internalize this reality and feel very far from reaching our God-given goals and aspirations.

When I came to Los Angeles to start my career, the entertainment world looked just as enormous as the Earth itself. It was intimidating. I remember spending so much time wondering how I would ever meet the people I needed to meet, how I could possibly begin to navigate a place that was so tremendous, and how I could possibly make the connections I needed to make in order to have the career that I believed God had revealed to me.

That feeling of being small in an enormous world finally led me to this chapter's Commandment:

Your World Is Smaller Than You Think

Have you ever heard of the concept of *six degrees of separation*? You probably have, but if you haven't, I'll explain. It is the theory in which none of us are more than six contacts away from anyone else on earth. The idea came from a 1929 short story called *Chains* by Hungarian writer Frigyes Karinthy. In *Chains,* one of the main characters challenges another character to find another person on Earth that he cannot connect himself to through fewer than five other people.

The idea remained fiction until 1967 when a Harvard psychologist, Stanley Milgram, attempted to test the theory from *Chains* in what became known as the Small World experiment. Milgram sent 300 packages out to people in Nebraska and Boston and asked them to use their networks to get them back to one specific target: a stockbroker living in Boston. They weren't asked to forward it to him directly, but to send it to someone they knew on a first-name basis, with instructions for that person to forward it on to someone in their network that they thought might know the stockbroker. Only sixty-four of those packages actually reached the target, but they took an average of 5.2 intermediary connections to get there. This experiment was used as evidence for *six degrees of separation,* or the "small world phenomenon," as the researcher called it.

In the fall of 2011, Facebook released findings from what was dubbed "One of the largest social network studies ever released." They reported that 92 percent of Facebook users around the world were only separated by four degrees—and when they looked only at users in the United States, it was closer to three degrees. Simply, the world isn't as big or impossible to navigate as it can often seem.

SIX DEGREES OF KEVIN BACON AND ZERO DEGREES OF YOU

Even before the Facebook report was released, I realized that the theory of "six degrees of separation" wasn't entirely true. You're actually a lot closer than you'd think to the people, opportunities, and experiences you need to advance in your life and career. Let that sink in for a moment. When you come to the realization that you're not as far away as you thought, that should renew your hope in what you're being called to pursue! When I realized that the distance between what I wanted to do and the people with the ability to help me do it was much shorter than I expected, that helped me aim even higher.

Back in the mid-1990s, a popular parlor game emerged called "Six Degrees of Kevin Bacon." Three Albright College students—Mike Ginelli, Brian Turtle, and Craig Fass—were in a heavy snowstorm and decided to pass the storm by watching television. One of the movies they watched was *Footloose* starring Kevin Bacon. Coincidentally, the next movie was *The Air Up There,* also starring Kevin Bacon. Intrigued by this coincidence, the three started counting up how many films Kevin Bacon had been in and how many actors he had appeared with on film. They quickly found that Kevin Bacon is no more than six degrees (shared movie appearances) away from indirectly collaborating with any actor.

While *six degrees of separation* is a cool idea and *six degrees of Kevin Bacon* is even cooler, they both leave out the power of God. When you factor God into the six degrees of separation idea what you come to realize is:

God defies the idea of any degrees of separation.

This means there are zero degrees separating you and your destiny when you allow God to guide you. Too often we don't rest in this truth. When we don't, it creates stress, anxiety, frustration, and even depression. Because we believe that we're so far away from ever achieving our hopes and dreams, we lose hope or become desperate. We torture ourselves with questions like, "How am I going to meet this person, and how am I going to network with that person?" After that, we start to strategize: "I must meet this person for my career to go to the next level. This person knows that person, so if I can get them to call on my behalf . . ." and so on. One of the problems with this approach (apart from the fact that it doesn't work very well) is that you run the risk of treating people like stepping stones instead of human beings—and run an even greater risk of revealing yourself as being an undercover opportunist instead of someone genuinely on a quest to fulfill their purpose.

I've learned that when you're operating in your purpose, using your gift, remaining pure of intent and passionate about what you have been called to do, *the right contacts will be drawn to you at the right time.* You don't need to obsess over networking or getting introductions from prospective contacts as a means to better your career. Being in the center of who God has called you to be and becoming great at what you do automatically draws people to you, no matter who they are and no matter what they do, even if they are some of the most influential people in the world.

I once had a chance to sit down with the legendary Quincy Jones, arguably the most successful producer in the history of music (he produced Michael Jackson's *Thriller* as well as my favorite film, *The Color Purple*). As I sat there talking with him, getting vital wisdom about how to be successful, I was feeling perplexed with my private career struggle. I was trying to navigate my own path to success while trying to position myself to be aligned with people who could help me. So, I decided to pick Quincy's brain on this subject. I asked, "How do you network? How do you get people to know who you are and help you?"

His reply was simple, profound wisdom that I have never forgotten: "You do the thing out of your thing and they will come to you!" What he was saying was, too often we put too much energy into networking and self-promotion and not enough energy into perfecting our craft. If you focus on your passion and become great at it, your work will become so compelling that people will have no choice but to seek you out.

I have found what Quincy Jones told me to be universally true. Some of my most important relationships didn't come about because I reached out. They came about because of the time, energy, and commitment I've put into my passion and purpose. That has attracted other people who share the same passion and purpose into my circle—and me into theirs. By pursuing what God called me to pursue in the way He called me to pursue it and trying to remain pure of intention, my work has been like a magnet that has drawn all sorts of people to me—and me to them. If you apply this in your life, it will work for you, too.

HOW I MET OPRAH

In the Bible, in Romans 8:28 (ESV), it says that "all things work together for good." Those are the perfect words to describe the incidents that put me on course to connect with Oprah.

It all started with a mistake. While I was still an executive for Sony

Pictures, a senior agent at CAA, one of the most powerful agencies in Hollywood, called my office and left a message that she needed to speak to me about a project. Because I was caught up in whatever seemed like a priority at the time, I didn't call her right back. Big mistake. When someone of that stature calls you, you return the call ASAP. Well, when I did return the call, she quickly pointed out the error of my ways. I felt horrible because my intention was never to be disrespectful. I immediately went into damage control and sent an apology gift to her office along with an advance copy of my forthcoming book *Produced by Faith*, just to say, "I'm sorry."

God has a funny way of turning our biggest nightmares into our biggest blessings. Months later, I got an email from this same agent saying she loved the book, and she thought it would be something Oprah would love too. She sent the book to one of the agents on Oprah's team, and almost a year to the date after I made the mistake I thought would damage my career, I was sitting down with Oprah Winfrey and her then–top executive, Sheri Salata, discussing my book and receiving the invitation from them to tape an episode of her world-renowned spiritual talk show, *Super Soul Sunday*. Mind-blowing.

This is why I believe that there are zero degrees of separation between you and your destiny. Even your mistakes will work for your good when you stay focused on what you've been called to do!

YOU NEVER KNOW WHO'S WATCHING

Now that you understand you're living in a small world, here's something else you should absorb and remember: you never know who's watching you. To put it another way, you never know who's being exposed to who you are and what you do. That's true not just in Hollywood but in any career and also throughout life. Even when you think you know, you have no idea of who's really paying attention.

That might seem ominous and intimidating, but it doesn't have to be. The reality is, even if you think no one pays attention to you or you're invisible to the powers that be at your job, you really aren't. You should behave *as though* people are watching, because they are. This means doing your best work at all times, of course, but it's deeper than that. You also need to be who you say you are, be true to the values you claim to honor, and stay committed to the purpose that God is calling you to. You never know upon whom your works, words, or actions will make an impact.

Word gets around. People pay attention to the good and the bad, especially when you stand out based on the quality of your results, the force of your personality, or your commitment to your values. Sometimes, when you're new and inexperienced in a company or a profession, it's easy to feel insignificant and frustrated because you don't always receive recognition for your efforts. Trust me, I understand, and I've felt this way many times. Yet this is when it's even more important to strive for greatness and push yourself to do your best because doing so helps you develop the habit of walking your talk and always giving 110 percent, the foundation of a sustainable and successful career.

Nobody will send a memo telling you that they are coming, but huge opportunities could be riding on what someone thinks of you, your skills, and your character. You might work under the radar for years and then one day get recognized, and suddenly everything you've hoped and worked for becomes a reality. So, act like you're always in the spotlight . . . because one day you will be. A life-changing opportunity could be around the corner at any time without you even realizing it. In fact, that's usually how it happens. Remember the words of Jesus, "Well done, good and faithful servant! You have been faithful with a few things; I will put you in charge of many things ..." (Matthew 25:23, niv).

INTEGRITY MATTERS

There's a word for displaying your character when nobody's watching and being the same person in private that you are in public: *integrity*. Being consistent in the faith you express in church and in the faith you act on the other six days of the week is another form of integrity. Both are about being consistent in who you say you are and the choices you make, and as a spiritual person seeking secular success, both are critical to your future.

Some people behave differently in public than they do in private and think they can fool people into believing they're someone they really aren't. Don't emulate them. You might fool people temporarily, but in the long run, you can do tremendous damage to your life and career if you think you can "turn on" decency, values, honesty, and piety only when you think someone is watching. That's a dangerous game, and as we've seen with political figure after political figure, to play it is to lose it.

I know this might sound strange given how Hollywood is portrayed in the media. The perception is that Hollywood is a place devoid of integrity, but this couldn't be further from the truth. In entertainment as in any industry, people want to work with individuals they can trust and count on. Integrity matters and its benefits far outweigh the temporary benefit of operating without it.

Integrity played a critical role back when I was developing *The Karate Kid* remake script. I had gotten into a situation where, because of my desire to service my ambition at all costs, I almost ruined my career. The producers of the movie had given me an early look at the first draft of the script and instead of giving it to my colleague who was working on the project with me, I gave it straight to my boss and cut my colleague out. To make matters worse, my colleague found out about it and went to my boss. I felt horrible and I immediately owned up to the error of my ways. I realized that I had done something that had violated who I said I was and what I believed in. I was ashamed of myself for allowing my ambition to get the best of me.

I was contrite, owned up to my mistake with my boss, and told him it would never happen again. Because I had built up a reputation as a person of integrity, I was fortunate: my boss gave me grace and didn't hold this momentary lapse of judgment against me. I was relieved and I fell to my knees and thanked God that I had received mercy when I didn't deserve it. Since then, I have worked diligently to ensure that my professional and personal behavior and my publicly stated values always align as closely as possible.

How often do we read about someone in the public eye who, behind the scenes and out of the spotlight, violates their public persona? History is filled with stories that illustrate the fact that what you do in private matters. *Integrity matters.* Integrity doesn't just show up as part of a presentation; it's not about convincing someone to think about you in a certain way. Integrity is who you are. It's how you live.

In Chapter Four, I shared the rules that govern every human enterprise, and you should probably add this one to that list: *Be a person of character and honor, even if you don't think anyone will notice.* Every industry is small. If you don't operate with a strong code of ethics, if you try to manipulate people or be one thing to one person and another thing to someone else, it will catch up to you. If you look at the long game, what happens to the cynics, the hypocrites, the people who cut corners, or who cheat? They go down.

In fact, there's a terrific scene near the end of the movie *The Big Short* where Steve Carrell's character, Mark Baum, perfectly expresses this idea to a group of Wall Street bankers on the eve of the 2008 financial crash:

> We live in an era of fraud in America. Not just in banking, but in government, education, religion, food, even baseball . . . What bothers me isn't that fraud is not nice. Or that fraud is mean. For fifteen thousand years, fraud and short-sighted thinking have never, ever worked. Not once. Eventually you get caught, things go south. When the hell did we forget all that? I thought we were better than this, I really did.

Integrity matters. Who you are in private matters, and not just because you never know who's watching. It's because integrity and character move even the most powerful people. I've seen it again and again in my career: you might think that my Sabbath observance would cost me opportunities, but it's actually opened doors. Why? Because people in any field, no matter how important they are, need other people they can trust. If you're a person of integrity, they know they can trust *you*. Even studio heads, CEOs, heads of state—everyone respects people of honor, character, and integrity.

You have to push yourself to be the same person at home as you are at work. The greatest benefit you will receive is *peace*. As I mentioned in *The Wait*, there's no peace when we're one person in public and someone else in private, because the two different people within us will be at war with each other. You only find true peace when you align your public and your private selves. Integrity equals peace and it also fuels something priceless and irreplaceable: your reputation.

REPUTATION IS YOUR AGENT

I've worked hard at trying to build a good reputation. My reputation has helped me benefit from amazing opportunities, has contributed to getting projects made and deals done, and has furthered my business. If you're in your line of work long enough, people will come to know who you are and what you stand for. You will earn a reputation, good or bad, and that reputation is more valuable than your work performance, box office receipts, or financial bottom line.

In fact, reputation is *everything*. Beyond having money, beyond having credit, the most powerful thing in Hollywood is reputation. Period. If you have a good reputation, you can get money. If you have a good reputation, you can get jobs. If you have a good reputation, you can get movies made. Your reputation is currency and it is the one currency that never loses value. Your reputation, like your brand, is a promise of what people can expect from you. If they know they can count on you being committed, passionate, ethical, and honest, you'll get plenty of opportunities. If they don't know what they can count on . . . well, you might find your cell phone very quiet.

How can you develop and maintain a good reputation in your business? Here are some ideas you might try:

- Don't compromise your values no matter how much pressure you're under.

- Don't take shortcuts in your work.

- Be mindful of how people perceive you and try to live up to their expectations.

- Have consistency between what you do and say in public and in private.

- Lift other people up as well as yourself.

- Hold superiors and employers accountable for their promises.

Mostly, be mindful and intentional. How did you handle the last project that you were on? How did you handle the last conversation that you were in? What did you do with the deal that you ended up getting? Did you make good on it? Did you not make good on it? And most important, when someone is asked about you, what are they going to say?

Your reputation is like your agent. When you are not in the room to speak for yourself, your reputation is there representing you. What will it say? What expectations will it create? I think one of the reasons I've been able to cut across so many industries is that I've built a strong reputation. I haven't done it by being who people wanted me to be, but by being who God has called me to be, and by trying to do my best to be a man of my word.

The thing about reputation is that there are no exceptions. In Hollywood or any business, it can be tempting to see someone with a bad reputation who's making big money and enjoying fame and think, "Why can't I do that?" But you have no idea of the price that person pays for the choices that led to that fame or fortune, day in and day out, in terms of relationships, health, and many other ways.

As people of faith, we should not uphold "getting away with it" as a standard of behavior. Faith stands for something, and that begins with me . . . and you.

False Idols

It's a high-wire act: caring about what other people say about you while NOT caring about what other people say about you. What I mean is, what others say is not the reward, and you shouldn't cater your choices to winning their praise. Sometimes what other people say can matter because it can be a reflection of how true you're being to the person God wants you to be. Evaluate the feedback you receive, yet don't make it the sole reason you make certain choices or take certain actions. Being true to your values and God's purpose should be its own reward.

IT'S TIME TO MOVE: PUT YOURSELF IN AN ENVIRONMENT OF SUCCESS

There's no question in my mind that if you act from a place of purpose, you will pull like-minded people into your orbit, even if they are people you assumed would never give you the time of day. However, as we've discussed, God only does his part when you do yours, and sometimes that means doing more than showing up as your best self. Sometimes, part of cultivating your purpose and passion means you must put yourself in the physical environment where the action in your field is happening.

Faith without works is dead (James 2:17)! But often I find that people of faith are crippled by fear of leaving the place they live in order to chase their dreams. You can't just dream about what you want; you have to wake up and go after it based on faith. There might be a certain thing that God can't do for you while you stay in the place where you grew up. Often times, doing what God has put in your heart requires a mighty move of faith—literally!

I'm from Northern California, yet Southern California is the entertainment capital of the world. I couldn't have found success in the career God was steering me to if I had been determined to stay in Oakland. I had to move to Los Angeles and put myself in the environment of Hollywood. It's very difficult for people to succeed in film or television if they don't live in Los Angeles, New York, or Atlanta (which has recently become a hotbed for production). It works the same way in many industries. You want to advance in country music? Ask, "What is the epicenter of country music?" It's Nashville. If you want to do big things in this genre, it's more likely to happen in Nashville. On the other hand, what if your dream is to work for a high-flying software startup? You probably need to buy a ticket to San Francisco and head for Silicon Valley.

I'm not saying that you can't break through in entertainment, ministry, or high tech without relocating; it's possible. But in my experience, it's a lot easier to find that next-level opportunity when you're immersed in the culture of your work day after day, surrounded by other people who are doing the same. Sometimes to be most effective, you have to put yourself physically in the environment of what you're aspiring to do.

Where do the best doctors normally come from? What schools? What areas? Go there. Wherever your industry is happening, wherever the people you're called to be working with congregate, go there. At worst, you go to New York or L.A. or London, and it doesn't work out the way you wanted. But you've had an experience that has made you better, matured you, and given you the confidence that you can try anything, go anywhere, and not only survive but thrive. That is a gift, and the only way to get it is to go for it. There is *zero* downside in trying to get closer to what God is calling you to do.

Hold on, DeVon, you might be saying. *I can't just leave my life and move across the country right now.* I understand completely. But there are situations where you will never know God's full intention unless you follow what He asks you to do, no matter how disruptive it might appear at first. That's difficult because nobody lives in a vacuum. We all have family, friends, and lives that we've carefully woven together, and relocating unravels them, sometimes beyond repair. Often, when God places that call in our hearts to follow His purpose, we don't do it because we talk ourselves out of it. Why? Fear. Fear is the biggest life and career disruptor. Fear causes us to rationalize and overthink.

When we're afraid, and we stay where we are instead of taking a risk and going where we believe we are supposed to be, we can miss out on the true fulfillment of our calling. Then we get mad, frustrated, or depressed that things aren't happening for us the way we hoped they would. Trouble is, God can nudge us to move, but He can't make us do it. If you hear the call to move in your spirit, don't suppress it. Consider that it might be time to answer the call once and for all.

If you've heard the call and balked at making the move, I want to remind you of something you may have forgotten. A lot of the time, we don't take that leap because deep down we fear that we don't have what it takes—that we can't actually make it in the field we aspire to be in. But when God is speaking to you with that undeniable urge to pack up, hit the road, and go where the opportunities are, He's also telling you that *He knows you can make it*. God doesn't do anything without an intention for success. If He places the desire to relocate in your spirit, it's because you have the strength, resilience, and talent to turn it into something amazing.

At one time or another, most of us feel the need to move, to go to a certain school, to change jobs, or to move to a different neighborhood. The recurring question we ask ourselves is: "How do I know if it's God or just my own ambition?" Whenever faced with an urge to make a move, I've asked myself the same question, and here are some questions you can use to help you decide:

- **How long have you had the urge?** Impulsive action is often wrong action, so it's important to look at how long the desire has been in your heart. A persistent urge that you can't shake is good evidence that it could be from God.

- **If you make the move, what are your motive and intention?** It's important to evaluate what you believe a move could accomplish and search your heart for your true motivation. Are you moving to achieve your purpose or for a more self-serving reason?

- **What does the cost-benefit analysis say?** Evaluate how much it's costing you to stay where you are (in terms of lost opportunity, advancement, and income, for instance) versus the benefit you're receiving from staying. If staying is costing you more than you're benefiting, it's time to move.

- **What does prayer tell you?** Ask God for wisdom, insight, and guidance on whether or not it's time to make a move.

If you trust God and you feel it's time to move, heed that feeling, even in the face of lingering doubts. There are certain things you won't get absolute confirmation on until you're in the environment that you're called to be in.

FAITH IS A SUPERPOWER

When I arrived at the historic Harpo Studios in 2012 to tape Oprah's *Super Soul Sunday,* I was nervous beyond belief. Thankfully, Meagan (who was my fiancée at the time) came with me for moral support. After a few hours prepping in the green room, the producers came and walked us to the set. I could feel my heart beating in my stomach. Then they announced, "Ms. Winfrey is on her way." Her arrival was electrifying: the whole set lit up, not because of the lights, but because of the power of her spirit. Her warmth and infectious smile immediately put me at ease.

As we took our places in two comfortable tan couch chairs, I felt this great sense of calm fall over me, and I kept telling myself, "God is with me, and even if I mess up, they can always edit that part out." The interview that followed was a kinetic spiritual experience; the flow between us was great. It was amazing! There I was, talking about my book with Oprah Winfrey! It was deep confirmation that God really is directing our stories because there is no way that would have happened if I hadn't made that first mistake. In the same way that Superman defies gravity by flying, faith empowers us to defy what appears to be the reality of our situation. Nothing is impossible to those who believe, and even the lowest plot points in our lives can be used to set us up for our greatest blessings.

The great wonder is, once you trust God as the unseen mover in your life, not only will things fall into place but you will actually begin to see your faith in a different way. Start asking good questions. Ask, "How do I walk in faith?" and "How do I listen to the Holy Spirit?" Those are just warm-ups. Ask, "How do I release myself from both the confining aspects of religion and what other people want me to do so I can do what God is telling me to do?" That's when life goes to another level. That's when you find your own superpowers and begin to "walk on water"—when you release yourself from preconceived notions of who you're supposed to be and who you think God is and trust in the moment. You trust who He is telling you to be and who He is to you.

As I've learned to walk in and by faith, I've learned that faith really is a superpower. It takes time to learn how to harness it and listen to

God, but when you finally get there, it's amazing what you can accomplish.

Why is this relevant to the idea that your world is smaller than you think? Because you're supposed to live a *big* purpose that has an equally big impact on a *small* world. Unfortunately, most people end up living lives that are smaller than what they are capable of because they never have enough faith to follow what God tells them through the Holy Spirit. In church, we are taught to listen to the Holy Spirit, but we have a hard time doing so when the guidance of the Holy Spirit challenges everything we think we know. So, we limit ourselves because we look at the world we want to enter—Hollywood, politics, sports, finance, you name it—and assume it's too big for us. We end up limiting the power of our faith. We shut off possibilities right away because we think pursuing something that appears so unlikely is an irrational act.

When we allow practicality and our dependence on what we see to talk us out of doing things that God is calling us to do—when we conclude that taking a leap of faith is an irrational act—we don't make changes that will improve our lives and careers. We basically proclaim that fear is stronger than God. Fear takes hold—fear that a risk won't pay off or fear that we'll be laughed at and humiliated for doing something that appears to make no sense. In order to take that risk and make that move, we need to understand this: making a life-changing choice based on God's Word is the *most* rational thing we can ever do.

How do we make faith a superpower? This is the process that most of the successful people I know follow:

1. Listen closely to God speaking in your spirit.

2. When what you hear or feel provokes a passionate response, pay attention.

3. Ask yourself, "What do I need to do in order to follow that God-given passion?"

4. Figure out the details and do it. Don't listen to doubters or nay-sayers.

5. Repeat.

Acting on faith is a habit-forming process. Once you do it and it works, the more you keep doing it. The more you keep doing it, the more comfortable you'll become doing it, and the more you'll trust yourself—and God. You'll find that using your faith can work more wonders for you than if you had Tony Stark's Iron Man suit!

Exodus

It's possible for your world to be too small. If you're in an environment where the unethical actions of others reflect on your reputation and make it harder for you to succeed (example: someone who worked at the corrupt energy company Enron might suffer a damaged image by association), it's time to move on. Staying is not an option because no paycheck is worth your reputation. When you take away titles and business cards, all you have is the answer to this question: "Are you who you say you are?" If your organization is affecting how others answer that question about you, get out. Fast.

DON'T BURN BRIDGES

My great aunt (and second mom), Aunt Donna, always told me "DeVon, never burn bridges, because you never know when you'll have to cross them again." These words would prove to be incredibly valuable in navigating Hollywood. There are bridges in every industry: people or opportunities that move you from one stage of your career to the next. Because Hollywood is such a tight community, if you stay in it for a few years, you usually end up crossing the same bridge multiple times.

This is why it's important to never make the miscalculation that, because you no longer have to deal with someone, you can treat them negatively. The next thing you know, years down the road, the very person you need is the very person whose bridge you torched while walking away like the hero in a bad action movie.

This reality plays out all the time. When I was an assistant and an intern, there were people who treated me very well. Now they're reaching out to me because they need jobs or connections—and because they showed themselves to be good people, I'm happy to help if I can. People who were assistants a few years ago when I was an executive at Sony are now running studio divisions, and because I was good to them, they take my calls and we work together. Never damage relationships intentionally. Never let anger or ego make you careless about someone else's feelings or reputation because you *do not know* how that person or project will play a role in your future.

Also, people only remember how things end, and I'm not talking about movies. No matter how great a run you've had with a company, when it's time for you to move on, people will remember most how you handled the exit. I've seen people leave jobs or projects in haste and hubris and turn what might have been career assets into detriments because they left hurt feelings or unfulfilled commitments in their wake.

Don't make that mistake. Do all you can to leave everyone with the impression that you are fair, committed, professional, honorable, compassionate, and kind.

Away from the Workplace

Dating is as much about reputation as it is about looks or personality. If you're faithful, word gets around. If you're a player who's taking late-night booty calls from a lot of different people, that gets around, too. Want to improve your prospects? Consider how people see you. Are you perceived as romantic and loyal? Or are they more likely to see you as callous and unfaithful? If your reputation on the dating scene isn't what you hope, what can you do about it?

HOW TO THRIVE IN YOUR SMALL WORLD

Those impressions have deep, lasting value because regardless of what profession you're in or what you aspire to do, you will need to meet people who can help you. You may need to relocate for an opportunity. You will definitely develop a reputation. Whether you will meet those people, make the right call about moving, and develop a reputation that makes good things happen will depend on knowing who God is calling you to be and being true to that person in everything you do and say.

Don't overthink this. It has nothing to do with Hollywood. Integrity and character spend the same whether you're in business, law, education, or any other field. So . . .

- **Take notes.** Keep track of the people in your world—what they're doing, where they're working, what they did for you, or what you did for them, anything that helps you follow relationships as they change over time. Whether it's a written journal or an online dossier, don't leave this to chance or memory.

- **Express gratitude.** This is such a basic skill that many people overlook it. When someone does something for you, thank them in a meaningful way. That does not mean sending them an email; anybody can do that. Express your gratitude in ways that mean something to the other person and take a little commitment on your part. Do the same when you fall short or offend somebody. Remember, my connection with Oprah (which has changed my life) came because I sent someone a book as a way of apologizing for my mistake.

- **Under-promise and over-deliver.** Quite often, people who are new to a company or a field will promise the moon, hoping to impress their superiors, then struggle to deliver. That's a recipe for a poor reputation. Instead, do the opposite. Make moderate promises and then work tirelessly to exceed them. That way, you're creating expectations and then exceeding them, which will help you build a reputation as someone who always gets the job done.

- **When in doubt, pay attention to your spirit.** You know what you stand for. You know what's ethical. The Holy Spirit is your moral, ethical compass at all times. When you're unsure about whether something you want to do (or have been asked to do) is in line with the person God wants you to be, trust your spirit. It won't steer you wrong.

Thou Shalt

- » Be honest. When you're truthful, you don't have anything to keep track of.
- » Network. There's nothing wrong with attending events designed to connect you with other people in your profession.
- » Pray. It's your guide and constant reminder of who you are and what you stand for.

Thou Shalt Not

- » Hold grudges. If someone wrongs you, forgive and move on.
- » Believe your press clippings.
- » Try to impress. Being who you are is enough.
- » Burn bridges.

EPILOGUE | **PEACE**

And this righteousness will bring peace.
Yes, it will bring quietness and confidence forever.
—Isaiah 32:17, NLT

When I closed my production deal with Twentieth Century Fox, I had to move off the Sony Pictures lot and onto the Fox lot. My office is on the twentieth floor of the Fox Plaza building, the same building where Bruce Willis shot *Die Hard*. My company logo is of a cityscape right at sunset with the initials FE on top of the words "Franklin Entertainment" between the city and the sky. One day, as I was moving in, I was getting my logo put up on the wall in my office lobby, and one of the guys putting it up looked out the window and said, "Look, it's your logo!" The sun was setting outside my office window, and it looked just like my logo rendered in real life.

I stood there in awe and I said to myself, "Look at God." It was a profound moment for me, a moment to reflect on this journey and all I've learned over the twenty years I've been in entertainment. If it wasn't for God's mercy and grace, I know none of this would be possible.

My goal with this book is to make it clear that by pursuing everything God has called you to pursue, and by doing everything He has called you to do in the world, you will not only achieve unprecedented secular success but also strengthen your soul. Despite what the people in my church said all those years ago, my soul and faith are stronger today because I've worked in Hollywood. I've seen what God can do when I've relied on Him and committed to the process that success requires.

I'm giving you strategies to achieve success in whatever business you're in because I believe that true success is a manifestation of purpose. Our purpose is the divine reason behind our creation. We weren't created to accumulate wealth, fame, cars, or houses. We were created because God wants us to serve a designated role in the world. That's a thrilling idea: that you and I have been asked to play a role in the work of the Creator. But in order to fulfill that role, we must fight to remain the person God created us to be.

Too often, anxiety impacts our lives and careers. Where is our place in the world? How are we going to get there? Why does it all have to be so hard? We have a desire to achieve success, yet when it doesn't appear immediately and easily, we become anxious. It's true: following the path to the career and life you are supposed to have is one of the hardest things you'll ever do. It's a trudge, and sometimes it feels like you're taking a step forward only to slide two steps backward. Yet, in the pursuit of the life we've been promised, there's danger in wanting success so badly that we will do anything to get it. "By any means necessary" doesn't apply if you're looking to achieve long-lasting success, because the means by which you achieve that success is everything.

OPPORTUNITY COST

This is why it's important to pay attention to Jesus's question, "And what do you benefit if you gain the whole world but lose your own soul?" (Mark 8:36, NLT). Granted, it's a disconcerting question. It's peculiar to talk about your soul in terms of profit and loss, so let's break it down. Whatever is left over of your gains after you factor in your cost, that is your profit. So, every bit of success you enjoy—a promotion, a raise, a story about you in the newspaper, an invitation to speak at a huge conference—has to be weighed against the cost. Did you have to compromise your beliefs to get it? Did you do something you vowed you wouldn't do? What does it matter if you've achieved prominence in the world but it damages your relationship with God?

In business, this idea is called "opportunity cost." Simply, what does each opportunity cost in terms of time, money, difficulty, or anything else that's valuable? If the cost is too high, even what looks like a once-in-a-lifetime gift may not be. So, as you journey into your career, as each new prospect comes your way, I suggest you ask, "What's the opportunity cost to my soul?" If it's too high, it's not worth paying. Remember, everything comes at a cost. Success achieved at too high a cost—your relationships, your family, your health, your peace, your integrity—is no success at all.

The thing is, it's not easy to turn your back on what looks like a transformative opportunity—something that on the surface looks like it gives you everything you've been dreaming about. That's why every step, every transition, should begin with intense prayer and a search for divine guidance:

Lord, show me the way.
Lord, please don't let me worship this.

Lord, please don't let me read my own headlines.
Lord, please don't let me sell the essence of who I am for a brief taste
  of success.

You don't need to gain prominence at the expense of your peace. You don't need to gain wealth at the expense of your health. You don't need to gain notoriety and respect at the expense of fulfillment and gratitude. So, what does it profit you to gain everything yet lose your soul in the process? Answer: nothing.

THE PEACE THAT PASSES ALL UNDERSTANDING

There is nothing in this world worth compromising your soul. There's a price to pay, not just in this life but in the life that comes after it. Think about all the people who gained worldly prominence at the cost of everything that really matters. Look what it did to their families. Look what it did to their children. Look what it did to their legacy.

Do not make success your God, or it will consume you. I see this dynamic play out in Hollywood all the time. I work in an industry that is fraught with myth and legend. It draws people like moths to a flame, and so do other fields: Silicon Valley startups, professional sports, medicine, law, and politics. People become desperate to be successful and get fortune, fame, and power. When they get it, all too often it changes them. They become people who will do whatever they can to keep what they have, regardless of the cost. When that happens, if they don't have a strong center of faith and purpose to steady them and remind them who they are, they can lose themselves. They begin to exchange pieces of their soul for pieces of whatever perceived benefit the world is offering. Little by little, their soul wears away until there's nothing left.

The other mistake that I see people making in pursuit of success is misconstruing the *trappings* of success for success itself. True success is spiritual; it comes with material reward, but it's really about peace, a sense of purpose and joy, and giving to others. It's not about the huge house, the expensive cars, or any of the other superficial rewards that some people think they have to indulge in to show the world that they're successful. At the end of the day, the peace that exists in your soul is the true barometer for your success. God will reward your good work with the peace that passes all understanding, and that peace cannot be achieved through material gain.

Peace is a magnet for purpose and prosperity. There's a great deal of baggage attached to that word—*prosperity*—but it's important to take a closer look at its meaning. Prosperity is simply the condition of being successful or thriving. You can be prosperous without money—and in fact, some of the most prosperous people are those with moderate incomes but healthy families, healthy bodies, and strong relationships with God. Money comes from fulfilling your purpose. You will fulfill your purpose when you fill your spirit not with anxiety but with the peace that comes from knowing that you are in the right place at the right time, ready to take the next step toward God's purpose for you. To sum it up:

Peace = Purpose = Prosperity

CHECK YOUR COMPASS

I'll admit it: practicing peace is hard. When we're on a career detour or when a plan isn't working out, questions like "When?" and "What if?" can become so loud in our heads that they drown out everything else, making it difficult to remain peaceful and trust that God is going to make everything happen for us as promised. Sometimes, despite my best efforts, peace eludes me, too.

When peace is hard to come by, don't go it alone. Finding success is like navigating a great sea in a small boat at night: you need a compass to find your way. Why do sailors check a compass? Because that's how you stay on course. If you don't keep an eye on your compass, you might end up somewhere completely different than where you intended—maybe even someplace dangerous. It is easy to lose your way. You've got to check back with that compass.

That compass is God. Check back in with your purpose every day. Are you pursuing what you want or what God wants for you? Are you being true to the person God created you to be? So many come to Hollywood with pure intentions and childhood dreams, and along the way, their values get corrupted because they've lost sight of their compass. Check in every day in prayer but also in honest self-reflection.

The thing is, even if you've lost your way, you can find your way back. Your gift, your talent—that's what you can go back to. Reconnecting with God can help reorient your direction and reposition you where you're meant to be. Be aware of who you are, be honest about your weaknesses, and remember that you were created to give praise, not receive it. Approach your success, and your journey toward it, with the deepest gratitude and thanks to God.

A MIRROR, KLEENEX, AND BAND-AIDS

Someone once asked me what it takes to make it in Hollywood. I think they thought I was going to say talent, passion, a dream, or something like that. But I replied, "You need a mirror, a box of Kleenex, and some Band-Aids." That's true whether you're in Hollywood or not.

You need a mirror because things will get difficult and you'll be tempted to change who you are. The mirror will remind you of who you are and why you got into whatever business you're in. You need Kleenex because you're going to cry. There will be nights that you'll be on your knees sobbing because you don't think your dream is ever going to happen. You will get passed over for opportunities, you will be frustrated, and you will want to quit.

Finally, you need Band-Aids because you're going to get hurt. People will talk about you, betray you, and even lie to you. So, you've got to be tough. When you get hurt, you slap on a bandage and keep going, all the while remaining exactly who God created you to be.

You will make it. I have faith in you. God has faith in you. Everything you're going through now has a purpose and is part of a journey God designed for you. As long as you remain true to who you are and make serving His purpose your real marker of success, you can't go wrong. I'll close with both a word of parting that means a great deal to me and a feeling that I hope God will grant you in everything you do.

Peace.

ACKNOWLEDGMENTS

I am eternally grateful for the all the tremendous divine assistance I received to help get this book to the world. I want to thank God and my Lord and Savior Jesus Christ for the opportunity to have had the experiences that provided the seed for the wisdom in this book. I want to thank my incredible wife, Meagan: you are a gift from Heaven. I want to thank the phenomenal Katy Hamilton and Harper-One family; my amazing book agents Nena Medonia and Jan Miller at Dupree Miller; my incomparable publicity team Joy Fehily, Cassandra Vargas, Caitlin Scott, and PMK-BNC; my friend and dynamic collaborator Tim Vandehey; my incredible social media team Jenn DePaula at Mixtus Media, Josh Chamberlin at Stickman Productions, and designer extraordinaire J. Q. Sirls; my marketing guru Rob Eager; my great friend and attorney John Meigs; my wonderful staff at Franklin Entertainment—thank you Ally, Ashley, Randy, and Kristina; and to my family, friends, associates, and fans—I thank you for your love, prayers, and support. I wouldn't be here without any of you.

READER'S GUIDE

1 YOUR PRAYERS ALONE AREN'T ENOUGH

1. How does the statement "Prayer isn't enough" make you feel, and why?

2. How has obsessing over results while ignoring the process hurt your career or other aspects of your life?

3. When did a difficult or challenging time prove to be your best training ground?

4. Name a time that God only answered a prayer after you did your part.

5. Name three ways you could boost your career through study and learning.

2 YOU ARE THE TALENT

1. Is your current career expressing your talent or servicing someone else's talent?

2. Can you think of a time when you've served talent but also been talent?

3. Talent is a validation of who you are. How does your talent validate you?

4. What can you do as a regular practice to keep your talent sharp?

3 YOU HAVE TO CARRY A CROWN BEFORE YOU CAN WEAR ONE

1. Whom did you serve to get into the position you have today? When you were in that situation, did you know how valuable the experience would be?

2. Whom are you serving? Whom should you be serving?

3. Have you ever compromised your faith-based values for a superior? Why?

4. What shortcuts—elevators—have you been guilty of looking for in your career?

5. If you found one, how did it affect your career?

6. Where is the seam in the field you want to be in?

4 YOU HAVE TO KNOW THE RULES TO PLAY THE GAME

1. Have you faced a situation where you helped a boss do something big but received no credit or reward? How did you handle the situation?

2. What expectations do you think you've created around yourself in your career?

3. What are the levers of power in your field?

5 YOUR GUT IS HIDING GOD

1. Have you ever felt God push you by finishing something you weren't ready to have finished?

2. Have you ever made a move without a safety net? Would you do it again?

3. Who could be a wise counselor who's at the career level where you want to be?

4. How could your church help you learn to trust and use your instinct?

5. What's your employer's attitude toward taking risks? Does it line up with yours?

6 YOU GET WHAT YOU NEGOTIATE (NOT WHAT YOU'RE WORTH)

1. How do you create value in your work? How could you let the world know?

2. Have you ever pushed back in a negotiation? Was the result what you expected?

3. What would ideal compensation look like for you?

4. What do you believe your worth is? Do you believe God values you in the same way?

5. Who could counsel you about a coming negotiation, and why would you trust them?

7 YOU MUST MASTER THE WALK OF FAME

1. Has your hunger for success turned into desperation?

2. Are you allowing your desperation for success to change who you are and compromise your beliefs?

3. Have you achieved a level of success that has brought some unexpected fame?

4. Are you confused about what should be the proper relationship between success and fame?

5. How do you deal with fame if it happens to you as a result of your purpose?

8 YOUR DIFFERENCE IS YOUR DESTINY

1. What makes you distinctive, and how have you been pressured to hide it?

2. Are you suffering from "sequel-itis," repeating failed patterns

in your life instead of trying something different? Why?

3. Is your process God's or your own? How do you know?

4. Do you fear criticism or seek it out? How do you make it work for you?

5. What could you do to keep your edge in your work and avoid the dangers of being careful?

6. Have you been servicing someone else's distinctiveness? Why?

9 YOUR AMNESIA IS AN ASSET

1. What are you holding on to that you should be forgetting? Why?

2. What should you be doing boldly instead of waiting for permission?

3. Are there transgressions you've not forgiven yourself for? Is it time to let them go?

4. What lessons and experiences do you not want to forget?

10 YOUR WORLD IS SMALLER THAN YOU THINK

1. How many degrees separate you from the people you need to know?

2. Who's watching you? Whom are you watching?

3. Are you resisting the call to move to an environment where success could manifest? Why? What will it take to make that move?

4. Have you burned bridges in the past? What could you do to prevent that from happening in the future?